BEHIND WALLS OF ST. JOHN'S

Library of Congress Control Number: 2017954229

Cover and interior design by Robaire Ream

ISBN: 9780988493858

BEHIND THE WALLS OF ST. JOHN'S

A Story of Catholic Abuse

Arlene Krieger

Minneapolis–St. Paul

Forward

C all it the hand of fate, or the fickleness of Mother Nature, or simply the pragmatic reality of statistics, but we are not all born equally. All of us are less than perfect when we leave our mother's womb. Each infant has a dual battle to fight; staying alive and learning how to cope with imperfection. The fight to survive makes us stronger and more determined.

Darwin postulates survival of the fittest. As the story unfolds, Darwin's theory is put to the test and redefined by the weakest of our society. In this case, the weakest, the children, become the strongest and eventually expose those who used their strength for evil. Forced to succumb to unspeakable acts, three-hundred young students found the courage and tenacity to survive crimes so heinous that they are unimaginable. Preying upon the precious innocent youth, what was perpetrated behind the walls of St. John's. It goes beyond civility; it emulates hell.

The story is not easy to read. It behooves society to record history so that these acts are never repeated. Sealed with the complaint filed in the State Court of Wisconsin were the experiences of some 300 complainants. This is the story of one of the 300.

Attorney Jeff Anderson became the crusader for victims of abuse from various churches within the Catholic Archdiocese. It was through him and because of him that nefarious behaviors of the clergy were exposed. Bursting the bubble of organized religion, he shed light on abominable abuses. Anderson's research uncovered a staggering number of victimized children before he filed the first complaint. There were more to follow.

The quotes used throughout the book are Carolyn's words as interpreted from sign language. I asked questions

1

and the interpreter signed them to Carolyn, who would sign the answers. The spoken word was then relayed back to me. To ensure accuracy, I asked the same questions more than once and always with another interpreter so the answers could be clarified as thoroughly as possible.

Carolyn kept thousands of emails. Some of them were signed to an interpreter and then transcribed. Because of Carolyn's education, her writing skills are at an elementary level. She signed to an interpreter who then typed the emails. It was the interpreter who took Carolyn's thoughts and put them in writing. She wanted to keep an accurate log of all that transpired. There were times when she was unable to find the right words and the interpreter assisted in recording those memories accurately. The majority of the emails were in Carolyn's own words and she hoped that one day a writer would take all those notes to tell her life story. It is the combination of those sources, the notes and Carolyn's words, that were used in writing this book.

For the deaf, the Internet has been the gateway to an entire universe that they would otherwise be unable to reach. Carolyn became adept at using the Internet and all it could offer. Self-taught, she explored topics until she found solutions. One morning I opened my email to find an inquiry about writing her story. I immediately replied and we set a meeting. When she arrived in a very old sedan, I wondered how she made the trip. What should have taken two hours took her six hours. "I had to stop for some food, go to the bathroom and buy gas," she told me. In reality, I doubt her car averaged more than forty miles an hour.

Carolyn was unable to read lips. We needed to communicate at an intimate level if the story was to come alive. Grabbing two pens and a ream of copy paper, we wrote down our questions and responses. The conversation was tepid at first, as Carolyn was testing the waters. She then motioned to her car. I followed her to the driveway and she popped open the trunk to reveal two blue plastic tubs filled with her life story. At that point I was unsure what the story was or if I would be able to write it. After dragging the two tubs into the living room we returned to the backyard and she extracted a letter from her pocket from her attorney, Jeff Anderson. Shaking her head in disbelief, she wrote, "This amount must be wrong." Once I read the short letter I was convinced she had a valid story, albeit a topic I had never referenced in any of my published works: pedophilia.

Pulling open the lids to the tubs she picked up newspaper and magazine articles, layers of pleadings, hundreds of emails and photos. A cursory review made it clear this was a story that deserved to be recorded, no matter how uncomfortable. Intrigued, I explained that unless Jeff Anderson gave his approval, I would not write her story. Experience has taught me to tread lightly when it comes to legal issues. After a quick call to the attorney's office, I received his approval. "In fact, I encourage my clients to talk about the experience," stated Mr. Anderson. "No one has told the story. Go ahead and write it. Send me a copy."

I began sifting through the tubs filled with documents. The dining room table was littered with pieces of Carolyn's life as I began to create some semblance of order. Once the writing process began we communicated through email, in person and via Internet interpreters. Carolyn would contact an online interpreter who would dial my cell phone. Carolyn would sign to the interpreter who would translate into the spoken word and vice versa. It was lengthy and arduous process, but these forms of communication insured the story would be told accurately and with the passion it so deserved. Patience and empathy were essential to completing the story. Like all serious writers, I immersed myself in the subject and found it almost impossible to endure. My mantra became. *Carolyn's story deserves to be told; I am responsible to make sure that happens.*

Chapter 1

Imagine you cannot hear.
Imagine you cannot talk.
Now imagine trying to communicate.

S he patiently sits at the window waiting for the mail truck to stop at the metal box. At the moment the postal delivery woman leaves, she extracts a key from the kitchen drawer and walks to the box. As she sorts through the various bills and advertisements, another wave of disappointment soaks into her mind. Nope, the settlement has not come through. In a somnambulistic state she returns to brood inside her modest home, the only one she could afford on her limited income. She could shed a tear, but experience has taught her that tears would do her no good.

Returning the key securely into the drawer, she hopes that tomorrow news will arrive and justice will be served. She opens the refrigerator and opts for a simple meal, gathering an assortment of fresh vegetables and a chicken breast.

The routine continues for days, followed by months and years. Her once thick dark brunette hair turns gray, her oval face becomes lined with age, yet she never loses faith in the power of Jeff Anderson, her attorney, her crusader in the fight to take back her life and announce to the world the crimes she had endured.

Winter never really arrives in the hottest city in America. It's rare when the air feels cool and crisp. Today Carolyn makes the daily trek to the mail box, a bit distracted from a gently blowing northern wind. It swipes across her face and teases her senses. Is the air playing tricks?

She browses through the assortment of mail and trapped between the water bill and a Macy's flyer is a thin envelope. Its letterhead reads, "Law Office of Jeff Anderson". Trembling with anticipation, she snaps the mailbox door shut, races home and rips open the thin envelope. It's the settlement letter. At the top of the page is the prestigious letterhead of the attorney's office, followed by a date, a salutation and just one sentence. "This is your settlement: please read, sign and return to our office." There is an amount highlighted in the middle of the page and at the bottom a signature line with a corresponding date.

Staring at the amount stipulated as her share of the settlement, she lets out a scream that would shatter glass, but she doesn't hear the scream. She only feels the omnipotent power of the law carving out her tiny bit of revenge. But it wouldn't have mattered if she received the entire settlement. No amount of money could have compensated her for a childhood stolen. Nothing on earth could have given Carolyn back all that was taken. The paltry sum of money does nothing to assuage her suffering or the anguish that haunts her heart and mind. Perhaps it can get her out of the tiny town and open new doors. No matter where she chooses to live, wherever she wanders, the nightmares are still lurking in her mind. They invade her sleep and steal pleasant moments. They seep into her consciousness when she eats. Will this pathetic sum of money buy her a bit of peace, a bit of sanity, a new way to live life?

Freeport, Illinois, is a typical Midwestern town in the heart of America. It's a sublime easy-going place, ideal for raising a family. Everything about the city reflects an intimate harmony with nature. The four seasons dictate the lifestyle of its 100,000 or so inhabitants. In the summer the sun glows brightly, casting warmth on the grass and cement streets, followed by cool northerly breezes drifting in to create fall. The rains are followed by snow and return to mark the beginning of spring. And so the cycle marches on year after year.

Margaret and Tony led the married life of the ubiquitous Catholic couple in the 1950s. Mass was celebrated in the household every Sunday morning as they marched off to church. Rigidly adhering to the laws dictated by the church, the couple dispensed with birth control and welcomed their first child barely a year after their nuptials. By any standards, they lived a modest, pious life. Tony was a skilled electrician and brought home ample income to sustain a family of three while Margaret remained home, devoting her life to their thriving infant, Marie Ann. Perfect in every way, the baby cooed her way into her parents' hearts. Swaddling Marie Ann in pink blankets, Margaret never left the home without her child. It was clear that she was filled with motherly instincts and bonded immediately with the infant, who became the love of her life and the apple of Tony's eye.

It seemed as though the very first night Marie Ann slept through without fussing or demanding a bottle, the couple took advantage of the opportunity and before their first child was a year old, Margaret found herself pregnant again. Financially things tightened up as the one income had to support a family of four. Tony was a drinker, becoming irritated and at times hostile toward his wife. Arguments were commonplace inside the wooden home which he had built with own two hands. Pride led to raw language and rough behavior.

A bottle of beer followed by another meant small disturbances would explode into all-out fights, the substance of which Margaret couldn't comprehend. Drunkenness had never occurred in her sheltered religious household and weathering Tony's wild spirit was challenging for this young mother. After his tirade, she would cry. Fraught with guilt, he would draw her close, they would reconcile, and nine months later there was another mouth to feed. Tom was the second child. Precocious in his boyish ways, he was the opposite of the demure sweetness of Marie Ann. Crawling at an early age, he got into everything and learned how to pick up a hammer and sling it over a piece of pine just like his dad. At every opportunity, he would observe Tony in the act of building and for a young child it all looked like a lot of fun. All that noise, all that hitting. It was the tools he loved the most—they were so powerful. Picking up a hammer, Tom found he could cause a lot of damage, much more so than if he just used his hands. To him it was all fun and games, as it should be for a young toddler.

Margaret's arms grew stronger as she wrestled to keep both children under control. Collapsing into bed each night, Tony reminded his weary wife that kids are kids–both were happy, healthy and normal. They should be thankful. Fondling her rosary, she admitted Tony was right. The Lord had blessed them twice with two healthy children. Tall and thin, she had to grapple with the fact her lithe body was slipping away with each birth, yet it never took away from her perfectly oval face, pristine cream complexion, and deep set round eyes. She was a beauty, a jewel for the eyes. Her thin long neck matched her thin long legs giving her the stature of Eastern European royalty. Yet as she closed her eyes, the regal blood flowing through her veins did nothing to temper the reality of a frenetic household. Praying for strength she asked the Lord to imbue her with the energy to run the home in a peaceful loving manner.

Margaret had taken Marie Ann and Tom to the park where they ran wildly from the swings, to the teeter-tooter, to the jungle gym. After an afternoon packed with physical activity, the children were exhausted. Margaret fed them dinner and they fell asleep earlier than usual. Tom was pleasantly surprised when he came home to lovely yet unusual silence. He took his wife in his arms and kissed her. He devoured the home-cooked meal and ended the evening with passion. A few months later, their third child was on the way. They prayed, as they had with the other children, that Carolyn would be delivered in perfect health.

Margaret couldn't help falling in love with the newest arrival who was the spitting image of herself; the oval shaped face, high cheek bones, deep set eyes—the infant was her mirror image. Like Tom and Marie Ann, she developed on schedule. She was in every way a blessed perfect child. Less stubborn than Tom and sweeter than Marie Ann, she became the shining star in a busy home.

A loud cry from the nursery startled Margaret out of deep sleep. It was Carolyn, and it was a cry more intense than she had ever heard. Touching the baby's soft face, it was damp and her forehead was burning with a fever. Bundling the baby into a blanket she woke Tony, ordering him to watch the other two children as she fled to the hospital. The on-call staff did what they could to save the infant's life but after several days the meningitis had left its mark—Carolyn became deaf.

A pall hung over the home and drastically changing the rhythm of the household. Their once docile sweet child, stricken with meningitis, became an unending source of tireless work, frustration and profound sadness. Communication ceased and the only sounds Margaret heard were the guaranteed whimpering and grunts of a sick and unhappy child.

Tom coped with the news the only way he knew how. Alcohol eased his heartache. He loved his youngest daughter but the lines of communication had closed and he was unable to find another pathway. Arguments were constantly simmering between Tony and Margaret. Tony would find any excuse to blow up, ranting over insignificant situations. Neither parent could find a way to cope so they took out their pain and frustrations by yelling and screaming at each other. Caroline was oblivious to the fighting and tension. When she was in her mother's arms she sensed she was loved and for a toddler that was enough.

Margaret was the last to join the family. Although Margaret never lost sight of her Catholic principles, she rebelled against the church's stand on contraception and began practicing a rudimentary form of birth control. Margaret learned to say "no" to sex when she was ovulating, and for

Carolyn at age three.

her it worked. She never became pregnant for the duration of their marriage.

The children grew tall, dropping one toy and grabbing another, replacing tricycles with bicycles, simple cloth books for hard covers, and babblings for real conversation. That is, all but Caroline. Unable to hear, her ability to speak waned and further affected her ability to communicate with the ones she loved. "I could see their mouths move but I didn't know what they were saying. I didn't know what they wanted and I didn't know how to respond."

Tony had had enough. It pained him to see Margaret's weariness. They had no way to learn sign language nor an inclination to do so. No one they knew had experience with this problem. There were no local community resources to assist them and if there were, the cost of the services would have been prohibitive.

He sat on the backyard stoop with a beer and pondered his life, his marriage and his children. Graduating high school by the skin of his teeth, he was cognizant that his relationship with Carolyn would never develop unless he put her education in the hands of professionals, those trained in teaching the deaf. All the prayers in the world would never restore his daughter's hearing. After three years of prayer and anticipation, Tony finally came to the realization that his daughter would never hear again. He wanted Carolyn to flourish like her siblings. That would never happen in their household. Where would he turn for answers? The only place he knew, the only place where he felt safe, secure, and loved. He turned to the Catholic Church.

Margaret's sister Tina walked into the noisy living room, shaking her head in amusement at the four children racing around the living room. Kissing Margaret's forehead, Tina held Margaret tightly. "I promise you this will all work out. You have faith in God and in Jesus and they will pave the way and shed light. Listen to your priest; he will give you the spiritual advice you are seeking. The Catholic Church has guided your life and it will continue doing so. Just follow the path your priest advises." Margaret loved and trusted Tina, and followed her advice as they grabbed their overcoats and trudged to the car for a meeting with the priest.

The room behind the pews was so dark that Tony knocked on the door to make sure the priest was inside. The lights flashed on, the door opened and the couple walked inside. They had never entered the private room and were fearful to speak—they didn't want to offend the priest, or God, or Jesus or any of the saints molded into the ceiling walls. A conversation of this magnitude began with a few deep breaths. Tony had been rehearsing this conversation for months. Tonight was his chance to say his piece and embrace whatever command the priest would offer for their deaf daughter.

"It's hard, not only for myself, but my wife and our kids. No matter how hard we try, none of us can reach our daughter. I believe the time has come to give her a chance to flourish. I believe, that is, Margaret and I, are holding Carolyn back. Our deaf child needs proper schooling and an education that reflects her inability to hear. We can't give that to her. We have come here to ask you to point the way, we have lost direction, we don't know…" before Tony could press forward with another word, he lost control and cried.

Margaret had never witnessed Tony cry, either tears of joy or tears of sadness. The priest, all too familiar with tragedy, gently handed Tony a box of tissues, stood up, walked around the desk and patted his arm. "With Jesus's help, we are going to make sure your little one finds just the right place." He returned to his executive blood red leather chair and pulled a pamphlet out of his desk drawer. Handing it to the parents he focused on their facial expressions. The priest was an expert in body language, well before the term became a popular phrase in psychological terminology. There was a crinkling of the forehead, an arch in the eyebrows, a shifting of the feet and when the last page was turned, a smile. They were convinced. What a deaf child meant to the church was another decade or so of tuition, money flowing into the coffers of the Catholic Church. In a subtle yet authoritative manner, the priest led a convincing discussion that would persuade the parents that he had found the solution to Carolyn's problem: St. John's School for the Deaf. It was a panacea, a haven to the children who were deaf and hearing impaired. It was not only the priest's answer, for that answer was wrapped around the Catholic Church, that answer included God, Jesus and all the saints that decorated the cathedral. The priest's decision was not one that he had made lightly on his own. Quite the contrary; it was backed by the sound spiritual expertise of the Trinity.

Thanking the priest, the young couple walked to the car and sat staring into the blackened sky. Tony had a clear definition of how to handle the situation but Margaret was torn. She began imagining what life would be without her beautiful child around the home. As a mother, she wanted what was best for her child, and she knew she was ill-prepared to teach Carolyn the necessities to forge through life; yet to give her daughter what she needed would mean removing her from the love of the household into a school that would provide her educational needs. The bond of love, ever so strong, was stretched so thin Margaret could hardly breathe.

In the end Tony won and they decided to place Carolyn at St. John's School for the Deaf.

Chapter 2

Piling the children into the back seat the family station wagon, they drove to St. Francis, Wisconsin, the home of St. John's School for the Deaf. Although Carolyn could not hear her parents speak, she sensed something was awry. Her siblings acted a bit odd, fidgeting in the car seat and opening their mouths wide; clearly, they were upset about something. After a long drive, Tony eased the car into a gravel parking lot. Carolyn looked out the window. The large stately brick structures loomed up to the heavens when viewed through the eyes of a small child.

St. John's School for the Deaf, Gym.

St. John's School for the Deaf, Main Building and Tower.

There were several buildings on the sprawling compound, all with designated functions, but it was the church that caught Carolyn's eye. It was so big, so old. It looked just like the church they attended each Sunday morning. Perhaps they were all going to a new church, she thought, but then her parents took Carolyn's hand and walked her over to a spate of nuns. Everyone was smiling and appeared welcoming. One of the nuns took Carolyn's hand and twisted her around so she didn't have to witness her parents racing back to the car and speeding away. The serenity of the moment was quickly shattered when the newest pupil let go of the nun's hand and raced back towards the parking lot. The car, her parents and her siblings were gone. Hysterical, Carolyn let loose her first round of tears.

At four years old, she had no coping mechanisms in place to understand or accept the disappearance of her family. All she had ever experienced was the love, warmth, and security of her parents and siblings, and in an instant it had vanished. The nun quickly retrieved the runaway, sharply grabbed her arm and marched her into the building that housed the youngest children. The spartan sleeping quarters were dark and there were two rows of cots lined up against the north and south walls. The nun set Carolyn's bag onto the cot nearest the bathroom and gestured, this was to be her bed and this was to be her home. Throwing a tantrum, Carolyn's recollection consisted of a constant flow of tears. She had no other way of expressing her feelings. Unable to hear, unable to speak, unable to communicate with the world, her frustrations were expelled.

The following morning, she joined other children on the playground and quickly realized, they too were unable to hear. At least there was one thing they had in common. With that knowledge, she had an inkling that she wasn't quite as alone as she had initially felt. Observing the children sign to each other, she quickly learned a simplified version of communicating and began interacting with some of her classmates. Although she was miserably lonely, for the first time in her life she felt as if she fit in with other kids, that

Sisters Claude, Bertrand, and Henriella.

her inability to hear was no longer a factor. For the first time, she was just like everyone else on the playground. But this realization never softened the memory of her parents abandoning her and she continued to sulk.

The nuns, her teachers, had no patience for Carolyn's behavior and began punishing her by swatting at her hands, and mouthing the words, "No." She couldn't hear or comprehend and continued crying. This behavior was answered with stronger slaps, which turned into harsh spankings. Of course, the more the nuns spanked and punished her, the more she cried.

When nap time arrived, the youngest children were led into the red brick building and told to lie down on their respective cots. The lights were turned off and the nuns retired to other quarters on the compound. Carolyn was too frightened to sleep but the rest of her classmates had fallen into a relaxed slumber. She couldn't hear the door open, but she felt a slight breeze as the wisps of the nun's habit passed the front of her cot—it was Sister Henriella. Carolyn knew she should follow suit and at least pretend to be sleeping, but curiosity got the better of her inquisitive mind and she squinted just enough to see why the nun had arrived. Several cots over, the nun walked to one of the sleeping young boys, pulled down his pants and began kissing and licking his penis. Startled, Carolyn's eyes opened wide. She was too young and too shocked to camouflage her feelings. What she observed was so bizarre, she had no idea what was happening. She was unable to judge the incident as right or wrong, good or bad. It was simply a foreign act. When the nun was finished, she looked up and caught Carolyn's eyes glaring in her direction. Instantaneously, Carolyn snapped her eyes shut, pretending to be sleeping. Although she could never erase the image, she was quite sure the nun was convinced that Carolyn was sleeping just like the rest of her classmates.

"I didn't know what to think. I didn't know if this was bad and if the boy was being punished. But I will never forget the look in his eyes. He stared blankly up at the ceiling and when the nun was done, she pulled up his pants and he rolled over on his cot and fell back to sleep. A couple of days later another boy and I were yanked from the playground and taken to the bathroom attached to the sleeping quarters. There were four nuns standing around looking at us. We were stripped from the waist down and given cold water enigmas. I screamed and screamed and cried. I didn't know what they were doing. I was scared to death. When they were finished with me, they did the same for the boy. If he screamed, I couldn't hear him. I was too terrified to move. When the punishment was over, we were returned to our cots. It was nap time."

It seemed an eternity before Carolyn could feel the warmth of her parents' arms. A full month had passed before the family finally arrived early on a cool Sunday afternoon. When she spotted her parents, she fled towards the car and Tony picked her up and held her tightly and then transferred her into Margaret's waiting arms. There were kisses and tears of joy spilt from their young daughter's eyes. A nun walked over, shook Margaret's hand and began discussing Carolyn's progress. None of this was understandable to Carolyn, she did not want her parents sharing a moment of their time with anyone else. Tugging on her mother's arm Carolyn mouthed the word "penis", but Margaret ignored her child and focused on what the nun was saying. Margaret was dubious that her daughter was trying to say the word "penis." *Where would she learn such a term? That word was never uttered at home.* Frustrated, Carolyn began to cry and refused to give until finally Margaret picked her up and placed her in the arms of her father. "I remember watching my mother talk to the nun. It had to be about me but I didn't know what they were saying. Mom must have been shocked at the word I used but I learned it from my classmates. The visit ended and like the last time, two nuns took my hand and distracted me while my parents left the school."

"The next day, I was taken to a room. It was completely dark, windowless and empty. The nun slammed the door and made me stay there all alone. I remember crying until the door finally opened and they set me free. It was like a prison, and it was terrifying. I didn't know what I had done to deserve such a bad punishment. I was too young to understand any of this."

The children at the school varied in the amount of hearing loss and in the amount of income. Those who were wealthier were treated far better than the poor children. None of the wealthy children were subjected to corporal punishment or sexual abuse; it was the poor kids who received the wrath from the nuns and it was the poor kids who stayed the weekends who received the worst wrath of all; sexual advances beyond anything Carolyn's mind could ever imagine.

"My cot was next to the bathroom and every Saturday evening the nuns would enter the bathroom and take baths. There was a tiny crack in the door and I remember watching two nuns kiss each other on the lips, and naked, watch them kiss each other's [genitals]. What I saw I didn't understand but intuitively I understood it to be wrong, simply because I had never witnessed such sights in my home. I didn't know if they saw me watching them, but I was punished again and again. One of the nuns would pick me up, throw me across her lap and paddle my bottom. Perhaps it was a blessing in disguise that I was unable to hear my own tortured screams."

"I felt so alone, especially on the weekends when most of the kids went home to be with their families. There were a few classmates left behind like me, but I didn't dare share the secret of what I saw in the bathroom. I didn't understand it so how could I explain it? I couldn't."

When Sunday morning rolled around, the youngest children, Carolyn included, weren't forced to sit through hours of worship. Instead, after a simple cold breakfast, they were ushered to the playground and remained there until the nuns retrieved them for the next meal. There was a set of monkey bars, a sandbox and swings, enough to keep the children occupied while the nuns tended to their devotions. The youngest nuns, novices, aged thirteen and fourteen, supervised the weekend kids. Their job was to guarantee they toed the line and behaved in a subdued manner. The problem with the novices was that they were unable to separate the brutality they had received at the hands of the older nuns with their job as loving caretakers to the youngest. Instead of compassion and love, the novices beat and abused their charges. Because they had never received compassion and tenderness, they carried out the same behavior and brutalized the children. Beating bottoms, pulling hair, punching, and slapping faces was how the novices dealt with what they deemed to be imperfect behavior.

That first Sunday after her parent's visit was the loneliest. It was hard to register the constant homesick ache in such a young child, the yearning for her parent's love coupled with the abuse she was receiving from her new caretakers. How does a four-year-old turning five, and eventually six, deal with such emotional atrocities? There are no words that can aptly describe the pain Carolyn was forced to endure. Per the advice of the convent, her parents stayed away for a couple of weeks to allow Carolyn to adapt to her new environment.

Monday morning classes resumed and she joined her classmates in play and study, but her mind constantly wandered to another place: home. Concentrating on the simplest task was arduous when her heart was filled with so much

Sisters Reynildis, Lounia, and Sophia.

emotional pain. During lunch period one of Carolyn's class-mates pushed her into a rock and her tiny finger spouted blood. Sister Reynildes was on duty and became extremely angry over the mess. "I was crying a lot and I remember they took me to the hospital and fixed my finger. None of the Sisters were kind. Sister Bertrand spanked my ass while my finger was still in a bandage and Sister Henriella pulled down my pants and spanked my nude bottom." The sim-plest accident on the playground was used as fodder for punishment. Instead of showing concern, nuns focused on what they considered behavior and doled out punishment in the form of sexual abuses.

One cannot crawl inside the mind of a young child, let alone a young child who is deaf, but one can envision the terror and helplessness she must have been feeling. She had grown up in a house filled with love, where a broken finger meant a trip to the doctor's office and a stop for ice cream to soothe the pain. It was a kiss and a deep hug that made the pain in the finger go away. That response was all Carolyn knew. But on the playground, when her finger was hurt, she was the recipient of abuse and disdain. Other than a patch-up from the hospital there was no care. How can such a young child cope with such drastic changes in behavior over the same incident? How was she supposed to reconcile this in her young inexperienced mind? The most probable answer was that she couldn't and she would become very confused.

Letters home were routinely written by the nuns to let the parents know how happy and well the children were. Each letter began with a crayon note from Carolyn, which was obviously copied from the blackboard. "Dear Daddy and Mommy, I am fine. We had fun, Love Carolyn." Then followed a serious note from a teacher. Sister Mary Bertrand wrote, "Just to reassure you again, please do not worry about Carolyn, if she is sick or something, we will be sure to let you know."

The nun's full-length habits held their sexual secrets and escapades. Back in the fifties, no one questioned the clergy, especially the nuns who had taken vows of chastity. The last thought on anyone's mind was that these devout members of the church would harm and destroy their young charges. Margaret and Anthony, as had all the other 300 sets of parents, put their faith in the church and its clergy. It was all they had to cling onto. Carolyn had salvaged several of their letters. Although the paper has worn thin and yellowed, the writing can still be discerned. The letters told the nun's version without an inkling as to the truth of what was going on behind the walls. No mention was made of sexual abuse, the punishments, the lack of caring and compassion, or the inferior education.

The days slowly evolved and the following Sunday morning Anthony and Margaret returned for another short visit. Carolyn's eyes lit up and her heart raced as she sprinted toward her parents. Anthony caught her in mid-air and held her tightly and then passed her over to Margaret. In Carolyn's young mind she knew this was it -- her parents were taking her home and she was ecstatic. After several moments, Margaret retrieved a large box of Italian cookies from the car and handed it to the nuns. Carolyn's hand reached up to grab her favorite treat but the box was quickly swept away. The cookies belonged to the nuns. Shrugging off the disappointment, she walked with her parents as they communicated with her teachers. Everyone was smiling and nodding their heads. From Carolyn's perspective, she was unable to grasp the conversation but she was quite sure it meant she would be returning home that very day. Why else would her mother be smiling?

It was not meant to be. Two nuns grabbed Carolyn's hand and walked her over to the playground. Placing her on a swing they distracted her as her parents walked briskly off the lawn and into their car. After a few moments, she jumped off the swing and ran to the spot where her parents had stood. They were gone. She ran around bushes and trees searching frantically for the family car and it too was gone. Throwing herself against the trunk of an oak tree she began to cry. Her parents had left her yet again. At best the nuns viewed the tears as a temper tantrum and responded accordingly. "I cried and I cried. I didn't want to be with the nuns. Martha [a nun] pulled me and then Sister Henriella hit my hip."

The photo shows Carolyn amongst the youngest students in the school. The backdrop sign reads, "Jesus Loves You," the catchphrase of the Catholic Church. Yet, it is highly unlikely that the parents of those innocent children realized that the catchphrases were expressed through the sexual abuses by the educators. The demarcation of sexual acts and emotional love became intertwined behind the vast brick walls. The educators saw no difference.

Despite being physically abused, Carolyn was not deterred from trying to survive. "I cried at dinner that Sunday evening." The heartache was so deeply entrenched and so pervasive, she had no other alternative to express her pain.

Yet on the way home, Anthony and Margaret reminisced over the short visit, filled with confidence they had made the right decision. According to the nuns, Carolyn was flourishing and making new friends. Her face always wore a smile (or so they were told) and she was happy in her new surroundings. The nuns described in detail all the wonderful things they were teaching the children but they left out the most important detail: none of the teachers were able to use sign language nor did any of the teachers possess a college degree. But Anthony and Margaret were not privy to that information. They took at face value the nuns' chronicle of a successful educational institution. Never once did the parents question in what manner the curriculum was taught or how the school conducted itself. It was a school run by the clergy who thought they were in direct communication with God and Jesus. It wasn't Anthony and Margaret's right to second guess the experts.

Returning home, Anthony relaxed with a few beers while Margaret told her three children about the wonderful visit. Marie Ann, the oldest, wanted to know all about the school and if Carolyn was happy. Mostly she wanted to know if Carolyn loved the cookies. 'Cookies? Gosh, Carolyn didn't get any,' thought Margaret.

Chapter 3

The presence of the school was punctuated by the yearly calendar; on all major holidays, the school was shut down and the boarders could go home. Unable to comprehend what the nuns were saying, Carolyn was overjoyed on that Wednesday afternoon when her mom appeared on the playground, placed her in the car and drove her home for the Thanksgiving holiday. This time it was tears of joy. Clutching her mom's hand, she couldn't get close enough. When Margaret needed her right hand to ease onto the freeway, Carolyn held onto her shoulder. Driving up the driveway, they were greeted by the other three siblings running out of the house. They encircled their sister, and gave her hugs and kisses on the cheek. So many words were coming from their mouths, but Carolyn understood none of them. What she did understand was that she hadn't been forgotten. That was enough.

Tossing her wool coat onto the bed, she felt her nose twitch as familiar aromas from the kitchen wafted into her shared bedroom. The room was just the same as the day she left, not one toy was out of place. Grabbing her favorite stuffed animal, she wandered into the kitchen and pointed to her mouth. She was hungry. Placing a snack onto the kitchen table, Margaret pointed to the wall clock and explained dinner would be ready soon. Carolyn smiled and greedily consumed the food, but she understood nothing her mother had just mouthed. An hour later, when the family sat down to the meal, she could put meaning into what Margaret had tried to communicate. Everything was so hard.

Seated at the dinner table with the entire family, she ate voraciously. The food tasted delicious; it was comforting. After gobbling down the last morsels on her plate, she returned to her bedroom to play with her long-lost toys.

Margaret came in kissed the girls goodnight, pulled back the covers, tucked them in. The two slept soundly for nine hours. For the moment, life had returned to normalcy. Carolyn was at home, with her parents, her siblings, and the familiar love.

Thanksgiving morning Carolyn rose, brushed her teeth and padded into the kitchen just in time to watch her mother insert a huge turkey into the oven. She threw her arms around her mom's legs and hugged her tightly. Closing the oven door, Margaret bent down and kissed her. How she had missed her daughter! Her beautiful, glorious, deaf daughter. The ache in Margaret's heart told her how much she had missed Carolyn, yet she knew she had to be strong and allow her daughter to receive the education she was unable to find in the public schools. The Catholic Church promised they would give her daughter the best education and all Margaret could do was put her faith into the church's promise.

Grabbing a frying pan, she scrambled two eggs and toasted an English muffin. Carolyn inhaled the food. The simplest things had gone missing since she was placed in the school. Hot food for breakfast was one of them. Later in the afternoon, Margaret's sister Tina arrived with her spouse Nick for the Thanksgiving meal. Tina was weighed down with gifts for the four children and Nick's arms were precariously balancing an array of baked goods. They exchanged hugs and took their seats at the elaborately set dinner table. Margaret lit three slim candles and the family held hands and bowed their heads. Carolyn couldn't hear Anthony recite the prayer nor could she hear everyone utter "Amen" in unison, but she could see the heads suddenly turned upright and hands reaching across the table to grab the serving utensils. It was time to eat.

Something was odd—her mother would always wake her and her two siblings and walk them to Sunday school while she prayed in the large chapel. Carolyn knew Sunday morning had arrived because her father was home, sitting at the breakfast table and reading the local paper. None of her siblings were dressed for church. The routine had changed and this was disturbing. There was a ring at the front door. Margaret's sister and brother-in-law had come to spend the day. The reason for their visit was to watch Carolyn's siblings while Margaret and Anthony drove Carolyn to St. John's. After several minutes exchanging hugs, Margaret held up Carolyn's wool coat, slipped her arms into the sleeves and the three of them entered the station wagon for the trip back to the school. The moment the car door shut Carolyn began to cry. Her tears continued until they came to a stop at the grounds of the church. Margaret was frustrated and drowning in guilt. She could do nothing to soothe or calm down her child. Clearly, Carolyn was out of control.

The nuns were ready with their usual condescending smiles for the returning students, assuring parents their charges would be well taken care of. When Anthony opened the car door, Carolyn bolted out and hid behind bushes and trees. At four she had little knowledge of self-preservation, and this was the only behavior that came to her mind. Crying didn't work nor did it give her attention. Eventually she was collected and returned to the living quarters. The nun pointed to the cot and made her stay on the bed. The loud cries landed on deaf ears, except, of course, the clergy. Margaret and Anthony had returned their daughter to a place that held nightmarish memories. They were clueless.

When a few of her classmates trickled into the barracks-like room, she rose from the cot and tried to communicate with them. Slowly, they taught her the art of communication through signing and slowly she began expressing her thoughts. The few children on the premises were served a cold, tasteless dinner and sent back to bed. Classes commenced in the morning. The next morning at breakfast Carolyn felt sick to her stomach, a tidal wave of homesickness enveloped her body. Staring at the bowl of cereal, she was unable to eat a bite. A nun came to the table and began admonishing her. Shaking her index finger, she placed her hand on Carolyn's shoulder, forcing her to sit and finish the bowl of cereal. The harder the nun pressed, the more hysterical Carolyn became. Turning her face towards Carolyn's, the nun pointed to the bowl of cereal and took the spoon and placed it into her mouth. The minutes turned into an hour and Carolyn was the only child seated in the dining hall. Finally, she forced herself to choke down the cereal and was released to the classroom. A few minutes later, she went to the bathroom and vomited. Homesickness was becoming her chronic disease with no cure in sight.

She felt like she was always being picked on and the first to be disciplined by the nuns. But on the playground later that afternoon, it wasn't so. It is not easy to explain why our minds remember specific occurrences and block out others. Perhaps the juxtaposition of returning from a loving environment to the spartan school made it easy for Carolyn to articulate the scene at the school yard. The early December sky was dark and foreboding but that didn't stop the nuns from forcing their charges to spend time on the playground. It was more than just Carolyn who was unable to readjust; several of the young boys were also acting out of line, at least in the eyes of the nuns. Carolyn watched as two nuns began hitting the boys while they were playing. "They would hit the kids while they were playing. The nuns kicked the kids with their feet and closed their fists and pounded some of the kids. I could hardly believe my eyes. My classmates were crying and running from the nuns. They were just as scared as I."

At the evening meal, Carolyn found it nearly impossible to eat. The ramifications of the afternoon beatings weighed heavily on her mind. "I was sick all day, every day. I never wanted to eat breakfast lunch, or supper. Sick! Sick! Sick! The meals were bad. Nuns told my mom I was sick all the time but mom told me to stay in the school." Carolyn had no ability to cope. Since she was unable to speak, write letters or call home, her parents were not privy to the inner workings of the school.

It was Sister Martha who stood out for so many years as a thorn in Carolyn's side. In the dankness of post-vesper prayers, the nun padded to the barracks and honed in on the youngest female: Carolyn. She bent down by the cot, and gently kissed the child's lips. Immediately, Carolyn's eyes popped open and she was shocked to see the nun next to her. A moment later, the nun put her hand to her mouth, which meant Carolyn must be quiet, and the nun lifted up her flannel night gown and began licking and kissing her genitals. After a short while, she pulled down the night gown, kissed her again and snuck back out into the pitch black.

How a young child responds to this behavior can never be fully addressed in the context of one succinct biography. Who could she turn to? Who could she tell? She instinctively knew the act was bad. Was it her own fault? Was she to blame for the nun touching her? Lying alone on the cot, her juvenile brain dwelled on the incident. She battled long and hard with the sexual encounter, but she was unable to come up with an answer. She had no way to protect herself against those adults, especially since they are part of the Church. The beginning of resentment toward her parents was planted in her brain. How could they allow this to happen? How could they put her in such an evil place? Maybe, just maybe, they didn't know what was happening. It would be up to her to tell them, but how?

She had tried and failed to run away. All that ever got her was locked up in the dark room. Panicked, she turned onto her back and stared up at the ceiling. There was no sleep for Carolyn that night. She was living in a hellish prison and from her point of view there was no way out. Five-year-olds contemplate survival, not suicide.

"Sister Martha continued to harass me constantly from the time I was four until I left the school at nine. All the girls and boys knew Sister Martha harassed me a lot." (At least that was how Carolyn felt.) The nun had found easy prey for her sexual needs and from that first evening, she never let go. Pedophilia took precedence over all of the nun's church vows and most importantly, her vow of chastity to her Lord.

A huge Christmas wreath adorned the front of the sanctuary to signal the next holiday and another chance to escape the school. Wrapped in her wool coat, Carolyn waited breathlessly for her parents' car. When her mom opened the door, she galloped over and hugged her. She had been rescued. On the ride home, she contemplated how to explain to her parents what was going on at the school. She was sure if her mother knew what was happening, they would pull her out of the school. She had to come up with a way to convince her mom. As soon as the front door opened, she ran to her bedroom and hugged Marie Ann, Linda and Tom. Home never felt so good and the smells wafting from the kitchen held the promise of delicious food about to be served. After a brief prayer, Anthony cracked open a beer and served up mashed potatoes, roasted chicken and hot buttermilk biscuits. Margaret watched her daughter inhale the food and then realized how very thin she had become. Holding up two fingers, she tried to explain to Carolyn the vacation was two weeks long. Carolyn merely smiled and reached for another biscuit.

The parents' frustration of being unable to communicate with their daughter became more pronounced as she became older. Neither noticed an improvement in her speech or comprehension. They had hoped after the first semester they would be able to hear their daughter say words, even the most basic, yet there was no indication she was grasping the language.

"After that vacation, I stayed at the school. I saw my mother crying. I cried a lot too. I remember my dad turning onto the school grounds and I saw the brown Ghost Building. The closer I got to the building, the harder I wept. My father came around and opened the car door and pulled me out. My mom was so thin, she was too weak to get out of the car. They just drove me to the school and dropped me off. The nuns would come and grab me, forcing me away from the car. All I remember doing was crying and crying. The nuns punished me with slaps and hits and spankings and then I just cried more."

To legitimize the school, St John's would often submit photos and articles to the local newspaper. This served to publicize their excellent work and of course to assist in obtaining new enrollments. A photo was submitted showing Carolyn as she dutifully learned how to speak by feeling the

Pupils Learn to 'Feel' Sound

An important phase of the teaching develops pupil's ability to recognize a spoken sound by vibrations it causes in teacher's jaw. Carolyn, 5, "feels" sound, repeats it.

sounds coming from the nun's mouth. The photo captured a happy child, fully engaged in the process of learning how to communicate. The caption read," An important phase of teaching develops pupil's ability to recognize a spoken sound by vibrations it causes in teacher's jaw. Carolyn, 5, feels sound, repeats it."

This false statement roused potential candidates into becoming future students and held the school as an innovator in teaching the hearing impaired. What the photo failed to show was that in fact that method did not work at all. None of the children learned to speak one single word based on that absurd exercise.

This photo was sent home to Margaret and Anthony so they too could see the remarkable teachings at the school. They thought, just look at the wonderful progress our daughter is making and it even made the newspaper!

"My mother wanted me to speak and the nuns told my mother that I would learn to speak." With the photo,

Margaret and Anthony had tangible evidence that in fact their precious daughter was learning to speak.

Another photo sent to the local papers was a demonstration of how fire drills were routinely practiced. The older students, dressed in uniforms, took the hands of the younger students and marched them down the steps. The young boy at the base of the photo, who appears to be crying, was the very same boy Carolyn had witnessed being molested by Sister Dorothy. Perhaps that explained his dour expression as he was led to safety. The caption read, "Fire warning comes from high pitched horn, much louder than usual fire alarms." Yet the irony of that caption, was the fact that this was a school for the deaf and the children would not be able to hear any sound from an alarm, let alone a high-pitched sound. In current society, all fire alarms are accompanied with flashing lights.

Even the most logical method of alerting the deaf of a fire was never implemented. St John's held itself up as a safe place to learn, but fell short when it came to safety. Observing the children marching down the staircase, none of them was aware an alarm was blasting away.

What Margaret and Anthony, as well as the other parents, were unaware of was the fact that none of the nuns, who were the teachers, or any of the clergy administrators were ever trained in teaching the deaf to communicate. There was not one college degree posted on any of the walls, nor any special degrees suggesting that anyone had ever studied teaching the deaf. Because the children had a wide range of the same disability, some of them could learn simply because they could hear the spoken word. Although Carolyn never heard a word, her colleagues could explain that the nuns talked very loudly, which allowed some of the children to capture the sounds and eventually the meanings. This was not so for Carolyn, who was completely deaf. St. John's had held itself up as an authority within the community and the Catholic Church when in fact all the school offered was a place to corral the hearing impaired. They claimed to offer a sanctuary for disabled children, children who did not fit into the public school system, children who were deprived of a chance to learn with their peers. The reality, as over 300 students testified to, was in fact merely a façade that camouflaged the sexual pedophilia of the clergy, from the headmaster to the novice nuns.

As the months passed it was Carolyn's classmates who taught her a rudimentary form of sign language and they became her only salvation in staying alive and keeping sane. Mimicking their behavior, she slowly tried to fit in. They accepted her. Eventually her parents stopped coming to visit on the weekends, as it became a horrific scene every time they departed. The outlandish tantrums Carolyn demonstrated and the wailing were too painful for the parents to endure. "When they stopped coming I thought my mom was too busy with my three other siblings to bother with me."

Lying on her cot, Carolyn prayed for help. One night, the nuns removed her from her bed, stripped off her clothes and gave her a bath. "Several nuns stood around me and were touching my backside and all over me in private places. I remember crying and thinking that this didn't seem right. My parents never touched me like that. Why are the nuns touching me like this? What did I do that was so bad to deserve this?" There was no answer, only terror. "They eventually wrapped a towel around me, put on my nightgown and put their fingers to their mouths, which I knew meant to be quiet, and walked me back to the cot."

"I had an older friend named Susan. We found common ground and I was able to communicate with her. She told me the nuns harassed me a lot more than the other boys and girls. She told me she watched the nuns hit me and she stood up to them and told them to stop it. The nuns slapped her face and in return she kicked them with her foot. Another boy also told me that the nuns kicked me more than any of the other girls. Part of the reason was that I was poor and had to spend the weekends at the school and another part of the reason was that I simply had no method of relating the abuse to anyone. My parents understood nothing. At least a couple of my classmates made me aware that they witnessed my abuse. I was no longer alone fighting that battle."

Joyce was another classmate who was privy to Carolyn's sexual abuse. "Sister Martha pushed Carolyn's pants off every morning and touched her genital area every day," remembered Joyce. "I told the nun to stop."

Chapter 4

T he weeks turned into months and at last summer arrived. Carolyn thought something was odd when the nuns retrieved her suitcase, opened it up, pointed and began filling it with her clothing. It wasn't the warm weather that clued her something was happening. It was that battered old suitcase. Observing the other children doing the same, she was quite certain she would be returning home. Later that afternoon, her parents arrived and did as she hoped. When she lunged into the arms of her siblings, she was convinced the nightmare was finally over. Her parents had made a grave mistake and had come to rescue her from clutches of the nuns.

"I spent that summer running around and hiding. My dad was always angry trying to look for me. I'm sure he was frustrated calling out my name and never getting a response. He drank a lot of beer and I would often watch his mouth move and his hands raise in the air. Even though I could not hear the words, I could tell he was fighting with my mom. It was upsetting to watch but there was nothing I could do. I loved my parents so much and it hurt me to see them hurting."

Almost every evening Margaret would gather the children and read a bedtime story. She would make them laugh and teach them new words as she flipped the pages. It was painfully obvious that her younger daughter Linda was quickly surpassing Carolyn's comprehension. Smiling and pointing to the words and the pictures, three of her children were engaged with the book. Carolyn smiled and watched her mom's finger pointing to the pictures. Perhaps this should have given Margaret pause that perhaps those promises St. John's had made were not true, but she fondled her rosary, and kept reading until it was time to turn off the lights. Who was she to question the Catholic Church? She had to be patient and give her deaf daughter time to soak in the new education.

Carolyn found love and security in the folds of her parents and siblings. When it came to physical attributes she was taller and stronger than the youngest. She could outrun, out jump and out climb Linda, but when it came to education, she knew she was lagging far behind. Her confidence waned as the summer weeks passed. Margaret and Anthony witnessed their daughter falling behind developmentally. When the summer ended, they packed Carolyn up and sent her back to St. John's. From their perspective, they had no other options.

She knew the road, the common signs, the buildings, the trees, the lush sprawling lawn and finally the gravel parking lot. The crying hadn't stopped from the moment Anthony inserted the key into the ignition until he opened the car door and dragged his daughter's wailing body from the backseat. The nuns were well prepared and stood strong and forceful as they approached the misbehaving child. As if on cue, they smiled, greeting the concerned parents. The second year of hell had commenced. Because so few children boarded at the school, Margaret and Anthony had not seen other children return to the school. They had no idea that Carolyn's emotional return was common. The nuns would shake their heads in disbelief at the child's behavior but after a short encouraging chat with the parents, they assuaged their fears. This was going to be the year that Carolyn excelled. She had a year under her belt and perhaps she just needed a little more time to adjust. It was Sister Renee who reassured Margaret that her little daughter was in excellent care and there was no need to worry. Patience was the mantra. Give Carolyn more time to adjust and learn the curriculum. Starring into the dark eyes of Sister Renee, Margaret felt compelled to trust her.

The predictable scene played out again. The screaming, the tantrum, the jostling to control an unruly child. Forming a tight circle around Carolyn, Sister Renee nodded and the parents spun around and walked to the car. Margaret cried all the way home while Anthony looked forward to the day's first bottle of beer. Another school year had begun.

In first grade, the children were not required to wear uniforms. The comfort of their own clothes gave them a bit of leeway in maintaining their individuality. For Carolyn, her clothing was a simple reminder of home. She could touch and smell it and feel connected. Monday morning the children were marched into their first-grade classroom. For some it was exciting, but Carolyn was fraught with anxiety. The nun pointed and each child was assigned a permanent seat for the duration of the year. After the nun led the Pledge of Allegiance, and morning prayers, the children took their seats and began what was supposed to be a stellar year in their educational development. The nun may have yelled, she may have wrapped the pointer on the desk, she may have mouthed instructions, she may have written instructions on the blackboard, but all this escaped Carolyn. She had no idea what was being conveyed. Her world, like for most of her classmates, was silent.

When the class stood up for bathroom breaks, she followed; when it was time for recess, she followed, and so on until the dismissal bell. Using her sense of sight, she was able to observe and copy her fellow students, which aided in demonstrating some kind of conforming behavior. She knew when the weekend had arrived—most of her classmates jogged off the grounds into the arms of their parents while she and a small group of boarders remained behind.

Friday night after dinner, the novices placed the children in their cots and disappeared to vespers. Once the solemn prayers had been recited, the second phase of the weekend commenced for the clergy, seeking sexual gratification at the hands of their young charges. "As in the past year, Sister Martha continued to kiss me every night and to touch my [genitals]. Sister Renee began fondling my chest. This time I fought the nun. I fought hard for her to stop touching me."

The harassment continued on the playground where all her classmates witnessed Sister Renee physically abusing her with slaps and kicks.

A few of weeks into the new year, Margaret and Anthony went back to the school. Once she was back in her mother's arms, Carolyn began a tirade. Carolyn did her best to convince her mom to take her out of the school. Pointing to Sister Renee, she began hitting herself and touching herself mirroring the way she had been treated. The nun immediately deflected Margaret's attention away from Carolyn's gesturing. After a lengthy consultation, Sister Renee convinced Margaret of her daughter's great strides, that she was speaking in the classroom and receiving excellent marks on her schoolwork. However, the nun never provided any examples of the well-executed work, nor was Carolyn able to spit out a single word; it was all left up to trust and blind faith.

"When I was six, Sister Martha and Sister Henriella told me I was sick. I don't recall feeling sick, but they convinced me otherwise. They pulled my bed [cot] into another room and when I woke up alone, I remember crying. I couldn't stop crying. I was in a small room and I felt scared. Later the two sisters walked in and began kissing me everywhere. I was shocked and kept on crying but it didn't stop the two nuns from touching me. It seemed like an eternity until the nuns were finished touching me and then Sister Martha brought in a big box of cookies and let me eat as much as I wanted. I begged to leave the private room and return to my friends. Pressing their index fingers to their mouths, as a sign to keep these things quiet, my cot was returned to the barracks and I joined my friends on the playground. The nuns seemed convinced the cookies would soothe me or perhaps erase the sexual episode but that didn't happen."

When I interact with Carolyn, she's staring into space, her eyes darted back and forth, flickering glimpses from the rotted wood floor up to the pockmarked ceiling. Her living space is in total disrepair, a hovel, not suitable for habitation, but this is where Carolyn makes her home. Her cats keep her company. Their love is safe, reliable and constant. It's the one thing she can rely on. As long as they have food, water, and a warm place to sleep, their devotion never wanes. Although Carolyn can't hear the contented sounds of purring or meowing, she feels their bushy tails rub up against her shins, their tongues giving an occasional lick to her cheeks. They will never abandon her—their love is unconditional, a love she had never had the luxury of feeling.

"I want the truth told. I want the world to know what those nuns did to me, to us. I know nothing can be undone, but if I tell my story maybe other parents will listen more closely to their children, maybe I can save another child from being sexually molested." Waving the settlement letter from Jeff Anderson, she adds, "This is not enough. No amount of money could ever be enough to undo the harm those nuns inflicted on me and my classmates. Winning a lawsuit isn't enough. None of the clergy were ever punished. They walked away with their pensions, their freedoms and their lives intact." Holding a colored photo in the air, she points to the blonde woman in it and signs to the interpreter. "This woman, the blonde, she was Sister Henriella. The nun who constantly abused me. See how she is smiling and so happy, her past completely forgotten? But I didn't forget and neither have all the other students who were abused by her. Free as a bird, she does as she pleases, her evil past completely erased. She was never punished for any of her deeds. None of this seems fair." At the end of our session, Carolyn waves goodbye to the interpreter and turns off the computer. Grabbing one of the cats, she walks to the backyard and breathes in clean, dry air. She forces herself to count her blessings, to thank God for decent health, and the chance to live out her life in a quiet peaceful setting. She wonders why now, at the age of seventy, she felt compelled to tell the story, the truth about what happened behind those brick walls at St. John's. Perhaps it was the victorious lawsuit won by Jeff Anderson that made the nightmare real, that told the State of Wisconsin and the Vatican all those sexual abuses were in fact real, not something conjured up in the minds of young deaf children. The win legitimized all the abuses that Carolyn and the hundreds of others had received at the hands of the clergy. The timing seemed to be right; with the huge settlement award, she felt compelled to tell the real story from the perspective of one young woman. "I can't speak for all of the others. Some don't want to talk about it, others have washed it from their memories. One thing I do know, when the 3oo students deposited the checks in their bank accounts, the ordeal they suffered will bubble to the top of their minds and they will be forced to recount a horrible part of their lives."

Taking a breath, she opened up the 23-year-old refrigerator, prepared a peanut butter and jelly sandwich and washed it down with a cup of ice water. The simple things in life brought joy into a life littered with so much wrong.

Chapter 5

I t came as no surprise when the end of the second grade wrapped up that Carolyn's teachers strongly suggested she remain behind. Conferring for a long time, the nuns felt it was in Carolyn's best interest to repeat the year. Not enough progress was made and it was crystal clear she was way behind her other classmates in all areas of academia. Pushing her to the third grade would only cause untold frustration for all concerned. Margaret and Anthony acquiesced to the nuns' advice and held Carolyn back. With blind trust as the parent's only tool, they never questioned the decision, nor did they bother testing their daughter. They grew to equate her hearing disability with an intellectual disability, which was absolutely incorrect; deafness is not an intellectual deficiency. The parents failed to see the problems with their daughter's education. The nuns placed the blame squarely on Carolyn's shoulders; it was she, alone, who carried the burden for her failure to keep up. Nothing was ever mentioned regarding the lack of communication or the teaching methods implemented by a battalion of uneducated clergy.

Suitcases appeared and she knew immediately the end of the school year had finally arrived. Gathering her belongings, she packed at lightning speed and joined her parents in the classroom. Her brightly lit face quickly turned dour as she observed the serious expressions on the faces of her parents. Something was wrong—she sensed it, she felt it. Tugging at her mother's arm, she begged to leave and, frankly, Margaret was quite ready to end the conversation.

Happy at home, Carolyn spent the summer playing with her siblings while Margaret spent the summer rationalizing and validating the decision of the school to hold back her daughter. When it came to physical activities, she was on par with her brother and sisters but not so when it came to basic reading, writing and arithmetic. It never occurred to the parents that they should independently test their daughter, that perhaps her failure didn't rest only with Carolyn, that perhaps the school was to blame. Clinging to her rosary, Margaret accepted Carolyn's fate and did what she thought was in her daughter's best interest. The parents discussed, and often fought over, how or if they should break the news to their daughter. Anthony's response was to pop open another bottle of beer and stomp off to brood in the backyard. Margaret did not want to do anything that would ruin Carolyn's summer, so she kept mute on the subject.

After several weeks at home, scrutinizing every move, Margaret observed that deafness didn't deter her daughter from holding a crayon and producing pages of colorful art. Carolyn could easily replicate letters and numbers with as much accuracy as their youngest child; it was her inability to communicate through speech that stymied the learning process. Margaret had no means to figure this out and thus she left this in the hands of the experts. With no options in sight, her only choice was to return Carolyn back to the school.

The process of educating the human brain is tricky. As the brain develops it creates elaborate pathways which accept new skills at precise times. If concepts are not introduced at those moments, learning becomes an arduous process and so it became for Carolyn and many of the other deaf children at the school. Repeating the second grade was not an ideal situation, but the school, with no tools to teach the deaf, chose to take the easy path and one that would add another year to her education and more money into the coffers.

When Carolyn walked into the familiar second grade classroom she looked around and noticed none of her classmates were around. Tugging on Sister Claude's habit she tried to ask her where her friends were. The response was a quick slap on the hand. Pointing across the hall, it became clear that Carolyn had been left behind. She was inconsolable. Her parents, her teachers, they had all lied to her. She fell apart. The nuns heard her screams and those were answered with several hours in the black dungeon. With the door forced shut, no one would hear the rantings of a seven year old.

After dinner, she joined her old classmates in the barracks as they communicated in their unique version of sign language. Finally, a smile appeared on her face as they shared stories of their summer. The topics were kept light and positive with the exception of Carolyn's horrible experience in the dark room. Her friends hugged her and vowed to help her through the year. When the novice came in and flipped off the lights, she had one positive thought to get her through the night.

In the light of day when classes commenced, so did the corporal punishment. Sister Bertrand relentlessly harassed Carolyn, particularly at meal times. The nun slapped and hit her until the plate was clean. On the playground, Carolyn watched Sister Claude kick an eight-year-old boy with her boot. It was so hurtful to see her friends being abused but at least she knew she wasn't the only student receiving physical abuse.

Aunt Tina came to visit several weeks into the school year. Carolyn's eyes lit up with joy when she saw her aunt walking across the schoolyard. Tina bent down and kissed her niece, hugging her tightly. After a few happy moments, Carolyn tried to communicate what was going on at the school, the sexual abuse, the physical abuse, and the dungeon. She began to reenact the behavior of the nuns. Using her tongue, her hands and her legs, she copied the acts of the nuns. Tina was clearly disturbed; she wasn't naïve and knew something was going on. Holding Carolyn tightly she shed tears. Carolyn's response was to beg Tina to take her home, far away from this ugly place. That was not Tina's decision to make and it tore at her heart to see her niece in such agony.

A novice was surreptitiously observing the scene and notified a nun. A sister walked over, introduced herself and Tina's attention was quickly diverted. Tina grabbed Carolyn's hand before following the nun as she escorted them around the campus. She chatted about the fine education and the wonderful teachings of Jesus Christ and then strongly suggested it was time to leave, as Sunday lunch was about to be served. Hugging her niece one last time, Tina returned to her car filled with sorrow. On her ride back home all she could think about was Carolyn's odd behavior, acting out scenes that were, at the very least, disturbing and sexual in nature; clearly something was amiss. She had no idea what she would tell her sister but perhaps she could drop a hint that other places might be a better fit for Carolyn.

Determined to pass the second grade, Carolyn made a concerted effort to behave, which meant following the nun's instructions and displaying effort in her schoolwork. Using her other senses, she did her best to perform at grade level. Using her eyes, she watched her teachers' every move and made sure her eyes were always looking squarely into her teachers' eyes. At the very least, the nuns would suppose Carolyn was engaged in whatever they were trying to teach. Her tactile sense was also heightened, allowing her the ability to feel things without actually hearing. The soft wisp of an overhead fan, the vibration of feet shuffling along a floor, the taste of a freshly baked cookie, the smell of chicken roasting in the oven, the chill in the morning air, all became pronounced, allowing her to experience a richer life. Leaning on her other senses she began to grasp more knowledge and slowly crept her way through the second grade.

With her eyes glued to the teacher, she learned to read facial expressions and to comprehend both broad and understated thoughts. Hoping her improved behavior would keep the sexual harassment at bay, she was sorely wrong. It didn't matter. "Sister Martha kicked my face and [genital] area every night." The brutality never ceased.

Several weeks later, the somber gray sky didn't deter Carolyn from the joy she felt when her mother walked across the sprawling lawn. Each visit meant salvation, a chance to run away from the daily nightmare. She sought refuge in her parents' arms; perhaps that was the day her mother would come to realize what was really happening. Carolyn clung to hope; praying to Jesus hadn't done her much good. After a moment of reconnection, Carolyn was dismissed so Margaret and Sister Ethel could hold a private meeting. Sister Ethel had learned of Tina's visit and was keenly aware that a seed of doubt had been planted in Margaret's head. It was paramount that Sister Ethel set the record straight. Kids act out and they take advantage of kindhearted souls, and Carolyn was simply milking her aunt for sympathy. With a condescending smile and a pious posture, the nun convinced Margaret that things were just fine. Retrieving a pile of school work, the nun held up the excellent examples reiterating the improved quality of Carolyn's work. By the time the conference had ended, Margaret was thoroughly convinced her daughter was thriving. They smiled as they departed the room, walked to the playground and observed Carolyn playing on the jungle gym.

In an instant, Margaret stood up and prepared to say goodbye. She refused to shed tears in front of her daughter. Holding a stiff posture, she hugged her daughter and purposefully strode to the car. It was time to go home. Before the first stop sign, she began to cry; she had doubts but no proof. Tina had suggested other schools but after making one heart wrenching decision to send her daughter away, doing it a second time might be even more painful. So she stayed the course, dismissed Tina's suggestion and kept Carolyn swaddled in the arms of the nuns.

There was a lot more going on than pedophilia. On the weekends when most of the children were safe with their families, the overnight boarders observed a variety of sexual behaviors. In the bathroom, Carolyn witnessed Sister Martha perform sexual acts with the other nuns. Unable to hear the cacophony, she had a clear view of what they were doing. She sometimes felt like the nuns were practicing on each other so they could pleasure themselves at the hands of the children. Through the eyes of an eight year old, none of this behavior made sense. She couldn't relate since she had nothing to compare it to. "I look, look and saw Sister Martha, Sister Henriella, and Sister Dorothy Mertens lick each other's mouth and their [genitals]. They were all nude. I watched this one Saturday night and then I shh shh. I went back to my bed but I couldn't sleep. In the morning Sister Martha's face was close to mine. She had a smile. Later I saw another private [scene]. Father Murphy, the headmaster and priest, was having intercourse in his private living room with Sister Lucina. Father Murphy did not see me. I walked softly to the bathroom. I was confused. I didn't know what sex was. I was shocked."

None of this happened in her own home. None of her family or friends ever displayed these actions. Coming to grips with such foreign acts, she was unable to cope or make sense of her life. There simply was no explanation and since her parents had no idea what Carolyn was seeing, they never came to her rescue.

As time wore on, she not only felt resentful but disconnected from her family. Unable to communicate the atrocities at the school, Carolyn was beginning to believe that her parents simply didn't care, which was the farthest from the truth. When Easter vacation arrived, she planned on making a concerted effort to explain what was happening. "When I went home I told Mom that the nuns were touching my bumps [genitals and breasts]. I tried to show her what they were doing but my mom didn't understand. I told my siblings I saw the nuns kissing and touching each other but no one seemed to understand." Defeated, Carolyn was unable to make anyone understand what was happening.

The children who boarded at the school were also experiencing these frustrations. Hundreds of other boys and girls found it impossible to relay the horrors of sexual abuse. Upon their return from vacation, each recounted how they had tried to reveal the sexual abuses and each was filled with the same sense of hopelessness. Deafness was not an invitation for abuse, nor did it mean the children were second class citizens, or without intellect or the right to live a peaceful, serene life. What it meant to the clergy was an opportunity to prey on the weakest and most vulnerable.

Carolyn closed her eyes and eventually drifted off to sleep. *Was there a God?* Because if God did exist he certainly wasn't living at St. John's.

At least one of her prayers was answered. At the end of repeating second grade, she was promoted to the third grade. Both Carolyn and her parents were pleased with her long-awaited progress. That summer was filled with the usual activities, except that she had taken the game of hiding to a new level. Finding every nook and cranny on the property, she could escape the world. When it was time for a meal or bed, calling out her name was useless, so Margaret asked each sibling to keep a close watch over their renegade sister, fearing she might fall asleep and spend the night in the dark. There was no doubt she could keep up with her siblings when it came to physical activities, but it was clear to Margaret that her reading and writing skills were slipping further behind. Carolyn was barely able to scribble even the simplest of sentences; nouns and a few verbs were all she could put to paper, and she was incapable of stringing together a cohesive sentence. Of course, this plagued Margaret's mind but then she would look around and for the moment she saw no alternative. When fall inevitably arrived, the familiar suitcase was put on her bed, but this year it was packed with a school uniform—a short-sleeved crisp cotton shirt, with a dark ribbon knotted at the neck, and a knee-length dark jumper. It was a step forward in growing up.

It was another year of abuse from various nuns. Sister Walter hit Carolyn as punishment for not responding to lip reading. Sister Ethel Strunk slapped her face and hit her behind her ears, just because. There was no real reason except to torment and abuse. Sister Ethel's favorite tool was a wood board that she would use to hit her hands or bottom. Carolyn received a stringent beating after Sister Ethel discovered a torn letter that Carolyn was piecing together. "Sister Claude put me in a cage. It was dark and it felt like a jail. I was totally alone for many hours. But I wasn't the only one. When I was released I saw Sister Claude put a boy in the jail. I cried and I screamed and I begged to go home. The nun picked up the letter, tore it into tinier bits and then proceeded on beating my hands with the wooden board. For sure the contents of that letter were never read."

Margaret picked up Carolyn on one Friday afternoon; the family was invited to a wedding and they were looking forward to a joyous affair. When she walked into her bedroom and spied a soft pink dress draped over the corner of the bed, she jumped for joy. Trying on the new dress, her mother brushed out her hair and tied a large pink bow around her curly ponytail. Looking in the mirror, Carolyn smiled at her reflection. She was beautiful, and for one moment she felt like a princess. It was a happy occasion and it felt good to smile, be with her extended family and eat great food. The fresh scent of the roses, the white tablecloths, the happy bride and groom, stirred feelings she had all but forgotten. In front of her stood a reminder of what the real world was like, that people could smile, dance, eat well and actually enjoy their lives. It wa a poignant example of the fact that normal life was passing her by. She was given a photo that she placed at the bottom of her bag. In it, she was smiling, wearing her new dress, standing next to her three siblings. The picture reflected a happy child.

Sunday evening Margaret and Anthony drove her back to school, walked her into the barracks and made the usual hasty departure. Changing into flannel pajamas, she extracted the photo and slept with it hidden underneath her pillow. The next day Sister Ethel discovered the picture and tore it up in front of Carolyn and then proceeded to chastise her for the frivolity. Shaking her fist, she scolded Carolyn for being happy. The nun pulled her hair and hit her behind the ear. Punished for having a good time, Carolyn learned a sorry lesson—keep her outside experiences hidden from the nuns. "I told Mom that Sister Ethel tore up the picture and punished me, but my mom told me to stop crying."

While the nuns were abusing Carolyn, they continued abusing numerous other boys and girls, zeroing in on the children who boarded over the weekends. One of the boys approached Sister Ethel and accused her of being a lesbian, and for those accusations he was beaten. He left the school shortly after. Apparently he was able to communicate to his parents what was going on. Sadly, the same could not be said for Carolyn. On another occasion she observed Sister Bernardio pull down the pants of several boys and spank their naked bottoms with a wooden board. The nun feared no repercussions from the parents since she was armed with a valid reason: the boys weren't behaving in the eyes of the Lord.

Around 1950 Father Gehl hired Father Murphy to run the deaf school, which gave him the opportunity to leave the campus on the weekends and live in his own home. Neither Father Murphy nor Father Gehl, had any training in teaching the deaf, yet they were in charge of the school, the curriculum and hiring the staff (who also had no training in teaching the deaf). Father Murphy drank a considerable amount of alcohol and never hid the fact that he smoked cigars. But what stood out in Carolyn's memory was his meanness. Walking the halls, he mostly sported a scowl. It was as if he was angry at the world and he took this out on the children,

Carolyn, second from right, age nine.

both in sexual and corporal punishments. "I was in Sister Renee's classroom when Father Murphy came in and closed the door. He came very close to me and hugged my face. I was wearing the school uniform and he put his hand up my dress and played with my genitals. I was laughing. He did this for an hour and then he looked at me and said he must go and that he was sorry for what just happened. My mouth remained shut. He did this again one other time. I was a little older and began to understand what was going on. I can't explain why I laughed. Maybe I thought that would stop him, but it didn't and he returned one more time to pleasure himself."

It seemed odd that Carolyn would remember how much time had passed, but there was a large clock on the wall and she could observe time ticking away. Perhaps that was the only real thing she had to cling onto as the priest fondled her private parts. He had no concern that he was destroying her mental health; he sought his own gratification and for him that was all that mattered.

Smoothing down her jumper, she wiped away the tears and joined her classmates in the schoolyard. What else could she do? No one would listen to her and no one believed her except her classmates. "Saturday afternoon, one of my classmates and I walked upstairs to Father Murphy's office and we saw him kissing Sister Lucina, on her private parts. Father Murphy didn't see us, otherwise I know we would have been punished. I was shocked. Another time I saw Father Murphy play with the boys. I watched him touch and play with their penises. I saw him having sex with Sister Lucia. I didn't understand what I saw but I knew it wasn't good and it wasn't right."

On a dreary spring Saturday, Aunt Tina and Uncle Nick paid a visit to their niece. When they walked through the schoolyard, Carolyn sprinted over and hugged them tightly. "I remember my aunt shaking her head in disgust and noticing that my clothes and body were very dirty. I begged for them to take me away, as I had done so many times in the past. I tried to explain how Sister Ethel had pulled my hair and pulled my tongue out of my mouth. I tried so hard to convince my aunt and uncle to take me away. I pointed to Sister Ethel and showed them what she did to me. I cried, I ranted, I grabbed my aunt and hid in her arms. Please let me go home! Please take me away from this school! I tried to communicate."

It was clear to Tina there were some real issues. Sister Ethel took Tina aside for another private conversation. This time, Tina stood her ground and said that Carolyn wanted to be at home with her parents. The sister reacted in a tough manner and explained that she could go home with her parents every weekend. As long as her parents arrived on Friday, she was free to leave the campus.

"I remember crying a lot, excited about the idea of going home every Friday night. At least I would have two days a week when I knew I would be safe and free from the abuses."

But none of that came to fruition. The following Friday afternoon when the other children stood in front of the driveway waiting for their parents to pick them up, Carolyn joined the group but Margaret and Anthony never arrived. Sister

Sisters Renee, Ethel, and Martha.

Ethel had lied. Dejected, Carolyn went back to the barracks and buried her head underneath the covers. And instead of lying in her safe, comfortable bed at home, she observed the weekend activities of the nuns. The bathroom door was slightly ajar and the lights were on. "I saw Sister Martha Ann and Sister Henriella [Dorothy Mertens] kissing, and licking each other's [genital] area. They were nude. I watched all night and then I quietly went to my bed. I couldn't sleep. All I could see when I closed my eyes is what the nuns were doing to each other. In the morning Sister Martha was standing over my bed, with her face close to mine and she was smiling. By now I knew what they were doing was wrong but there was nothing I could do or say about it. I was just happy they were so busy with each other that they ignored me."

Sometime later, when Carolyn was almost 11, Sister Henriella repeated the same acts on Carolyn that she had witnessed between the two nuns. Carolyn was taking a bath and Sister Henriella crept into the bathroom and proceeded to rape her while she was in the tub. The nun grabbed at the child's breasts and inserted her fingers into her vagina, all while smiling at her subject. She never gave a thought about robbing Carolyn of her childhood. All that mattered was satisfying her own sexual desire. She stole the carefree happy life every child should be allowed to live. She preyed on the fact that deafness had rendered the child incapable of communication and that these abhorrent acts could forever go unnoticed.

The daily routine at St. Johns continued on as if nothing foul had occurred. When the children were promoted to higher grades, additional chores were added to their schedules. They swept the floors, cleaned their rooms and the bathrooms, did the laundry for the clergy, scrubbed the basement floor and picked up debris on the playground. It was the job of the students to keep the campus spotless, a job that was never mentioned to the parents when entering the school. The nuns would keep a watchful eye on the slave labor, admonishing them if the work wasn't up to their high standards.

"I was often sick and spent a lot of time in bed," Carolyn remembers. That was one way she coped with the abuses. It is nearly impossible to describe what was streaming through Carolyn's mind: terror, fear, horror, shock, anxiety, frustration, and emptiness. No matter how many times she begged and pleaded, Margaret and Anthony were clueless as to what was going on at the school. Anthony could not cope with the constant tears and tantrums. Instead he drank more and ignored the rantings of his deaf daughter. As the years passed and her writing and communications skills plateaued at a third-grade level, her parents should have been alerted that something was awry at the school. Between Anthony's drinking, the constant fighting, and the other children, they didn't open themselves up to what was happening to their deaf daughter. There were too many other distractions.

No one knew what was going on except her classmates, who were sharing the same ordeal. Although Carolyn could commiserate with her classmates, it never served as a defense against the constant abuse. "When our parents would come to visit, the nuns would tell them lies, that we were all getting an excellent education and that we were happy. I was so angry because we were not believed. I suffered so much."

Chapter 6

I t was Marie Ann, the oldest sister, who finally began believing her sister's horrific story. Several years older, she attended a college located close to St. John's. One weekend she decided to surprise Carolyn and pay her a visit. On the short trip she envisioned the smile on her sister's face. She also envisioned another ranting tirade of how she wanted to go home, how miserably unhappy she was and how much she missed their parents. Putting those thoughts aside, some quality time was well worth it. The sun was brilliantly shining with a slight westerly breeze, the sky was azure blue and cloudless. Walking over the plush grass, she spotted her sister lounging on her cot, sound asleep. Gently waking her, Carolyn's eyes bulged open when she stared into Marie Ann's face. Jumping up, they hugged and began conversing as best they could. Finding a piece of paper and a pencil, they communicated back and forth by writing. Marie Ann wrote in complete sentences and Carolyn would respond in cryptic staccato words. Shaking her head in disgust, the older sister, now embroiled in college material, realized how far behind Carolyn had become. Incapable of writing more than a three or four-word response, the education she was receiving was inferior. She knew Carolyn wasn't dumb, in fact she was clever, creative and sensitive, but the education she was receiving did not cater to her needs. Carolyn would tug at her arm and try to explain that the nuns did not know sign language and because of this it kept her years behind her intellectual abilities. Marie Ann was not the parent and all she could offer was love and caring. On that lovely Saturday afternoon, that was enough for Carolyn.

They began wandering around the campus. It was still, quiet, serene and seemingly peaceful. There were a few students meandering around the main chapel cleaning the pews and preparing for Sunday Mass. Carolyn introduced her sister to everyone she met. She was proud of her older sister and the fact she was in college. As they approached Father Murphy's private office a nun whisked by, her face flushed and her habit disheveled. Clearly she was in a hurry. Carolyn gently knocked on the door and Father Murphy, who was aware the children could not hear his commands, got up and opened the heavy oak door. His face was also red but he sported a smile when he saw Carolyn. She turned to her sister, and Marie Ann introduced herself. The room was filled with educational books, stacks of letters, assorted bibles, and numerous pictures hung on the walls. In the corner was a small fully stocked bar with several crystal glasses on the counter top. He was prepared for visitors. He motioned to the two tapestry chairs in front of the large mahogany desk and they sat. Carolyn watched as the two chatted for a while and then he came around the desk and touched Marie Ann's arm, smiled, arched his eyes and drew close to her face. She was taken aback when Father Murphy began to flirt with her. His gestures bordered on too familiar. They quickly departed his office and Carolyn continued with the tour. Stepping into one classroom, Marie Ann was surprised at the lack of books and tools. The room was austere and dark. Reviewing

Father Murphy, center, receives donation check in 1966.

the few books on the nun's desk she noticed there were no books that alluded to sign language, the primary tool needed to communicate with the deaf. The afternoon disappeared and Marie Ann had to race to grab the last bus back to her campus. Hugging her younger sister, she galloped out of the classroom and sprinted to the bus stop. She had a date and was looking forward to a great evening.

On the ride back to campus, she ruminated over Father Murphy's flagrant flirting and the years of Carolyn's tantrums, wondering if perhaps there was some validity to her constant misery. It was time to place some doubt in her mom's mind. The combination of an inferior education with the possibility that her sister was sexually abused set her mind in a tailspin. She would find a private moment, sit down with her mother and make her listen to reason. This was not a conversation she wanted to have but after brief exposure to possible sexual harassment, it was time to talk to Margaret. As the oldest sibling, she felt responsible for her younger sister. If what Carolyn had been trying to communicate for almost a decade was all true, then Margaret and Anthony would have a heavy debt to pay to their child. Guilt was just the tip of the iceberg.

In the upper grades, Sister Wilma Fairbanks doled out a series of failing marks. "I fought with her all the time. She gave the kids who had the most money the best grades and me the worst grades." The reality that Carolyn's writing and reading skills were inferior compared to her other classmates hadn't crossed her mind. She tried, she concentrated, but Sister Wilma's instructions were next to impossible to understand. By now several grades behind in writing and reading, she was unable to comprehend what was being instructed. The nuns taught lip reading but Carolyn never caught on. She needed sign language.

While Carolyn was struggling, Marie Ann talked to Margaret and Anthony. Quitting college, she packed her bags and came home. It just wasn't for her; she had bigger things on her mind. She began explaining her suspicions about St. John's and that Carolyn's horrific rantings had validity. She elaborated on the meeting with Father Murphy, the classrooms, and the behavior of the other children, but mostly she discussed her sister's behavior. She portrayed all the symptoms of a sexually abused child (that Marie Ann had learned about at college). "We have to do something before it is too late," said Marie Ann, fully aware that the situation was beyond too late.

The next day, Margaret took the family car and brought Carolyn home. She began asking questions. "Sweetheart, did the nuns bother your hands, face, arms, hips, and legs?" Margaret had no idea how to broach the subject of sexual abuse. Using the word 'bother' seemed to be plain enough for her daughter to understand and respond to.

"I shook my head and mouthed yes, yes, yes! Then I saw my mom and sister talk a lot more. I could see the upset expression on my mom's face. Finally! She finally believed the truth! After a while my mom and sister hugged me. That was my last day of torture at St. Johns. Sister Thomasilla Michels and Sister Wilma Fairbanks called the house and requested a meeting with my mom. I knew that they were afraid the truth had been revealed. The sisters told my mom and dad that I wanted to stay at the school and that I was doing so well. I went to Confirmation Day, packed my bag and left the nightmare. My mom was really mad, mad at the nuns. I believe the happiest day in my life was that day."

Dressed in a white confirmation dress, Carolyn, at twelve years old, joined her classmates in the May ceremony. She said goodbye, snapped the door shut to the car and never looked back. Thanks to Marie Ann, her woeful cries had been heard and answered. Maybe God did exist.

The sexual predators at St. John's School for the Deaf were real people, committing heinous crimes which took decades to uncover and expose. How was one young woman supposed to get her day in court, a chance to be heard, a chance at restitution and a chance to right a wrong?

It would come but she would wait decades for her prayers to be answered.

Chapter 7

Anthony felt the need to begin again. Mentally and physically worn down, he wanted to provide his family with a better situation. Margaret investigated alternative schools and located a school for the deaf in Oshkosh. Although this meant a move, the family rallied around and looked forward to the fresh start. As a certified electrician, Anthony found a job in Oshkosh before the For Sale sign could be removed from their old home. They squeezed four kids into the backseat, loaded up the car and drove to their new home. The streets were lined with trees and perfectly manicured lawns. "The houses were good and it seemed like a rich neighborhood."

Anthony slowly eased the car up the driveway of a 1920s Victorian home. The front walkway was thick with low-lying bushes, and tulips sprung from the flowerbeds surrounding the front of the home. Walking up the little steps, they admired the wide porch and stepped inside a tiny foyer leading to the first level. The high ceilings made the home feel spacious, and the oak floors and large brick fireplace made it seem warm and welcoming. The kitchen had all the latest appliances, all in white, a brick floor and tiled countertops. Peering into the modern double oven, Margaret turned to Carolyn and mouthed that she would teach her how to make all those cookies she loved so much. Opening the side door the children ran to the sprawling backyard. The grass already needed a mowing and the flowerbed was overgrown with healthy weeds among the patches of multi-colored roses.

The children marched up the steps to the second floor and scattered into their bedrooms. Every room was filled with sunlight, ample space to sleep, closet space and study areas. All those new sights and smells flooded Carolyn's senses. For once everyone seemed to be filled with joy, and any dour expressions were melted away. It was time to begin anew.

Margaret supervised the movers while Anthony drove off to his new job. It seemed with all those old homes, electricians were in high demand. He put in as many hours as the company would give him and often worked overtime on the weekends. If nothing else, it left little time for his excessive drinking.

The children, now out of elementary school, allowed Margaret time to begin her own career and she opted to study nursing, another in-demand job. At 45, she enrolled in college, worked hard and graduated in two years. She had no trouble finding a job after graduating at the top of her class. They had finally become a two-income household. The fights over money were finally over. They had more than enough to cover all the essentials while living in a beautiful home in a safe neighborhood. Margaret's ambition served as impetus to Marie Ann, who also returned to college, eventually earning a Master's degree.

Carolyn spent a content and carefree summer in the new Oshkosh home. Inhaling the new smells, the new sights, and the new tastes, everything was fresh and she felt safe and secure. The only worry was sharing one bathroom with the rest of the household. Her parents enrolled her in the Oshkosh School for the Deaf. It was a large facility built in a brick and mortar English style. The classrooms were large, filled with sunlight, books, and the latest technology. When the secretary took them on the tour she couldn't help but notice that Carolyn was opening every door and closet. "What is she looking for?"

Carolyn responded, "The cell, the black dark jail where they put you to be punished." She was terrified of being punished in the same manner she had become so accustomed to. The secretary shook her head 'no' explaining there wasn't anything like that punishment in the school. As she set the new student's mind at ease, she noticed Carolyn stopped opening every single door. Carolyn observed janitors instead of young students cleaning hallways, as well as the spacious classrooms, individual lockers, a large cafeteria, art rooms, science rooms, and a huge library. This was a grand school, and for once her worries of sexual abuse were put to rest. Her body shook with excitement and anticipation; here was where she could finally get an education, learn to communicate with her family and have the chance to become someone of value.

She was both anxious and excited as her mother dropped her off at the new school. Wearing a new dress with a matching yellow bow tied to the side of her wavy blonde hair, she looked adorable, especially while wearing a genuine smile. She first sat in the classroom apprehensively, but using her other senses she observed her classmates and did as they did. Her teachers had received her transcripts and were aware of her skills and the inferior education she had received. They were determined to bring her up to speed; it was obvious she had suffered and deserved a fair chance to become educated. At this school sign language was the main form of communication and it was clear the newest student had years of catching up to do.

And so she began anew, making friends and interacting with classmates, doing all those activities that everyone else took for granted. On Saturdays she met her friends at the mall, watched movies, went bowling, celebrated holidays, took bike rides, hiked around the lake, ice-fished, ice-skated, and went to parties. Living every moment as if it were her last, she began to realize how much she had missed and how much more to life there was to experience.

Her main goal was succeeding in school and her classroom behavior was exemplary. Focusing on the teacher and her classmates, she tried earnestly to complete the work at her best ability. Luckily her friends and teachers were patient, offering kudos often. Margaret and Anthony were thrilled with Carolyn's progress. Each morning their deaf daughter woke up happy, looking forward to another day of school. Wearing new clothes and boasting a wide smile, the once miserable child morphed into a well-adjusted freshman. They knew they could not undo the past. All they could offer was a chance at the future. Sharing a rare kiss at the breakfast table, the parents knew they had made the right decision moving to Oshkosh, as everyone in the household seemed to be flourishing in the new city.

When the school year ended, Carolyn was promoted to the next grade, but her teachers explained that she was still several grades behind. Psychologically it was in her favor to promote her to the next level to be with her classmates, but she needed a great deal of tutoring to catch up. The parents took this to heart and encouraged their daughter to spend time in the public library over the summer. The school had given them a list of programs that would help her with reading and writing skills. When she returned in the fall, she had made gains and although she was still behind, slowly she had worked toward closing the gap.

Margaret took her growing daughter shopping for new school clothes at several of the family-owned businesses on the main street in town. They selected new dresses, a warm wool coat, and new underwear including several bras. "You are really growing up. You look beautiful!" Kissing her on the cheek, they stopped at a soda shop for a hamburger and milkshake and walked several blocks home. Carolyn never let go of her mother's hand. In that moment, she felt safe, secure and loved. It seemed after a decade apart that those warm fuzzy feelings would never return, but her heart soared with warmth. She loved her parents and tried to wash away all those ill feelings of abandonment.

It wasn't paradise. Those sporadic moments of comfort weren't as frequent as the nightmares. In the evenings, when she shut her eyes, a decade filled with sexual abuse invaded her dreams. The beatings, the sexual molestation, the constant fear of the nuns surfaced each and every night, waking Carolyn up with panic attacks. She constantly wondered how her parents could have given her up to St. Johns, how they were unable to understand what was going on, how they ignored her pleas and desperation. The life she was living in Oshkosh should have been the life she was living all along. Why did they wait so long? Those were questions that a young child was unable to resolve alone. Those gruesome memories would force themselves on her the rest of her days. It wasn't like there was some magic wand that could swish all those experiences away; no new house, new room or new neighborhood could undo the evil forced upon this young child for ten long years. She had no choice but to learn to live with the hellish memories.

It wasn't fair. Some of the most vulnerable among us in our society were the chosen prey of the Catholic Church. At such a young age, retribution never crossed the pre-teen's mind, but one day it would catch up. One day she, along with several hundred abused children, would take a stand against the heinous crimes. For now, Carolyn would try to make the best of her new life. She was thankful things were turning around, thankful to be home with her family, thankful for being loved, thankful for warm good food, for a new school and friends. That was her fresh start.

All went well in her first year at Oshkosh School for the Deaf. She struggled, but for once Carolyn was looking forward to going to school. The teacher was kind, considerate and patient and she was free of sexual harassment. Reticent, she treaded lightly, completed the homework to the best of her ability and always paid strict attention in class. She did not want to give her teacher a reason to discipline poor behavior. By all means, she was a good student but she struggled to keep up in English and communication skills. Her best subject was math. In many ways it made sense as math is nothing but symbols and signs, and those she was able to comprehend. She learned the basic facts easily and was able to string together simple algebraic equations; to her way of thinking it was logical. Her teacher rewarded her efforts, and encouraged the good work. At least the teacher had some basic training in teaching the deaf and knew how to extract the best from the students.

All in all for Carolyn, the first year was an excellent experience. She learned that there was such a thing as a caring teacher, that she was capable of learning and developing, that she could make friends and do all the normal activities that kids her age were doing. Life seemed to fall into place.

When the first bell rang in her sophomore year, she found herself in Mr. Becker's homeroom where she would be spending the day learning the basics. Similar to the other classes, this room held more books and a greater variety of novels and biographies. He would be teaching all the core courses including science, math and art, but the majority of her day would be spent on communication skills, an area where she was lacking. Early in the school year, Mr. Becker pulled Carolyn aside and signed that he wanted her to remain after class because he felt she needed extra guidance. She immediately replied 'yes' and at the end of the school day, she remained behind. Mr. Becker walked her toward the back corner of the room, brushed her hand with his hand and told her she was cute. He said he wanted to help her through the school year. He gave her an easy novel and told her to read it over the weekend and then they would discuss it the following week. With that short interval, he quickly released her and wished her a good weekend. At first she was flattered. He was tall, nearly six feet tall with wavy brown hair. He had a straight medium build and was handsome by a conventional standard. What Carolyn did not know was he and Father Murphy had grown up together in Milwaukee and they were on confidential speaking terms. As a young hopeful student, she reflected on the flirtatious incident and wondered why she was a target. After learning more about the situation, it became crystal clear that Father Murphy had relayed his numerous sexual encounters with Carolyn, marking her as an easy target for other teachers.

This overture caught her completely off-guard. Was this sexual harassment following her wherever she went? Mr. Becker simply brushed his hand over her face; there was no real sexual touching, but would this gesture evolve into something more? Where could she turn to? It seemed too early in the school year to eke out advice from fellow classmates and if she complained to her parents, they would think she might be making this all up. Could this possibly happen more than once in a lifetime? So, she did as the teacher asked. She struggled through the novel trying to comprehend as much as she possibly could. At that point her reading skills bordered on fourth-grade and this was a sixth-grade book.

Mr. Becker waited until mid-week when he again asked Carolyn to remain after class. She was well-prepared as she held the novel tightly in her hand. Again, he walked her to the back of the room, looked intensely into her dark eyes and assigned her questions about the book. Satisfied he was truly interested in her intellect, she had made an attempt to understand most of the written words and respond to his questions. But then his actions progressed from a caring doting teacher to a sexual predator. He brushed his hand against her face, drew her face towards his and he began kissing her lips. She pushed him away, but that didn't deter him from reaching underneath her dress and fondling her genitals. Again, she pushed him out of the way, hit his arms and raced out of the classroom. Tossing the book on the ground, she ran to her locker, grabbed her coat and stumbled home. Her cries were not heard, her voice was mute, but the tears coming down her face were clearly visible. Opening the front door, she raced upstairs, flung herself on the bed. For a rare moment, the house was empty. Her parents were both working and the other siblings were out of the house. She took a shower to wash Mr. Becker's memory off and then crashed onto her bed to mull over the situation.

It didn't stop, not for Carolyn nor for other girls in the Oshkosh School for the Deaf. After several months of continued sexual fondling she discovered she was not the only young teen subject to Mr. Becker's abuse. "He had sexual relations in the hallways, in the bathrooms, the locker rooms and the classrooms. He even invited the boys to come and watch as he had sex with me and other girls at the school. Once I remember Mr. Becker was fondling me in the back of the classroom and he invited the boys to come and watch. I remember the boys saying it was a sick thing and they didn't want to watch. I don't know how the teacher's behavior could have been kept a secret. I had to endure this for two years until I finally left the school at fifteen."

Carolyn befriended Alice, aged fourteen, who was also a victim of Mr. Becker's. The girls became close, enjoyed each other's company and shared one dark secret. Alice's situation became dire as she found herself pregnant. When Margaret, Carolyn's mom, complained bitterly to the police, they refused to intercede; there was no legal help for Alice. Devastated, eventually both girls dropped out of the school and went their separate ways. Back then paternity tests didn't exist, and neither did the rights of the young students. They endured whatever was doled out from their teachers, who ruled the classrooms with unabashed freedom and, seemingly, immunity from the legal repercussions.

This time when Carolyn bitterly complained to her mother about Mr. Becker's behavior, she listened. Not only did she listen, but she took the time to investigate and found out that Carolyn was not the only recipient of the teacher's sexual harassment. Margaret took the time to meet with the teacher and argued about his obscene behavior. Because of the dearth of laws, Mr. Becker was never prosecuted. The police did nothing to stop the rapes and sexual molestations of the young women. They all just stood by and allowed it to happen until one day, he left the school.

One Sunday a deaf schoolmate came to dinner and admitted to Margaret that the teacher had kissed her and was forward with sexual advances. This sealed her belief that yet again, Carolyn was subject to sexual advances and she allowed her daughter to leave the school at 15. Several other young girls also departed, but nothing was ever done to punish Mr. Becker's predatory behavior. As much as Margaret complained to the police, they explained that they had no jurisdiction over internal school affairs. Teachers were revered and respected in the community and the police did not want to upset the apple cart. There were simply no laws in place to protect the students' rights. They suffered in silence.

It seems incredible that our American society in the 1950s was so unwilling to protect our children. Their place held so little value that laws were never put into action to protect the most innocent part of our lives. The answer may lie when one looks back to the political leaders, all males, who thought the job of protecting children was for mothers only. But that changed when women returned to the workforce, leaving children more susceptible to abuse from caretakers. Shortly thereafter, laws were created to protect the young from sexual predators, including teachers and clergy. It was a long time coming for American society and way too late for many young boys and girls.

Chapter 8

It was agreed that Carolyn would leave Oshkosh School for the Deaf. After the sexual molestation incident, Margaret learned to trust and honor her daughter's wishes. Carolyn would leave the school without a high school degree, which would make earning a decent wage difficult. The one subject she enjoyed was math and she was also proficient at copying. The answer was a special vocational rehabilitation school in Milwaukee. In order to attend the school, Carolyn had to move out of the house and live on her own. After the trauma the household had suffered at the hands of schools, Margaret and Anthony decided to go along with any decisions Carolyn made. At 15, she packed one bag and moved into a one-room apartment in Milwaukee, not far from the school. During that time, a high school diploma was unnecessary to be accepted into the program and so she, for a small tuition, was enrolled. After reviewing the courses, keypunching seemed to fit her proficiencies. Since she was good at copying, and had knowledge of basic math skills, it seemed the best choice. Although none of the teachers understood or used sign language, it was unnecessary for learning the skills.

She studied diligently, gleaned all the basic applications and maneuvered skillfully around the keyboard. That was the coming of the computer age and anyone who could accurately keypunch was guaranteed a position upon receiving a certificate. For once, she was relaxed in her classes. What the other students took for granted, she did not. When a teacher approached her, she froze, but as time evolved Carolyn realized the teachers were there only to teach with no other agenda. For once, she let down her protective shield and she was able to keep up with the class work. She was motivated on many levels; she didn't want to be a constant liability to her parents, she wanted to prove she could be independent, and she wanted to prove to herself that she could make a living and be good at a profession.

In spite of her traumatizing encounters with men, she befriended a handsome young student. She and Gary met at school and became good buddies. "I didn't have that many girlfriends; I found it easier to have boyfriends." At 15 they dated casually, spending Saturdays together. "I remember we walked to the lake and he kissed me. I was upset and shortly after that we broke up." First loves are pointedly remembered. The relationship lasted but a short couple of months, yet the memories stayed in her heart forever. If nothing else Carolyn's confidence improved since a boy, her own age, could genuinely care for her.

Shortly afterwards, Carolyn met Dick, a teenager from Oshkosh, who fell madly in love with her. They dated for three years. Dick's mother was not at all pleased with the situation and when it came time for prom, she demanded that Dick ask his former girlfriend Elaine to attend. He obliged his mother but admitted that he didn't love Elaine. He lied to Carolyn about it. She was heartbroken, screaming out that Dick's mother didn't want her son to be with a deaf person. Not only did Dick escort Elaine to the prom, but he proposed and three months later they were married.

"I loved Dick, he was so handsome. He broke my heart." When things didn't work out with the young newlyweds, he came running back to Carolyn. "I said, 'no' I am finished." Suffering another heartache with Dick would be too painful. Luckily, there were a lot of other young men around who found Carolyn attractive.

There was no doubt she was popular with the boys; she was in fact a natural beauty. Standing nearly five-feet-six, with baby blue eyes, thick blonde wavy hair and a svelte shape, she was stunning. For many young men, when her only flaw was deafness, it was often overlooked; she had too many other assets that made her an intriguing and desired young woman.

Emulating her sisters, she learned how to apply makeup, dress in flattering clothing and create different hairstyles. In short, she learned how to attract men. Between her natural beauty and all those helpful hints, she never wanted for a date.

During Carolyn's three-year stint at the vocational school, she studied a plethora of disciplines and when she graduated, she would finally have her high school diploma. The school was extraordinarily kind and allowed her to bring an interpreter into the classrooms; in fact, she was the very first student who used an interpreter at the school. Because she was so far behind the other students, the vocational school allowed her to simultaneously attend a local college where they tutored her in reading and writing skills. This was the main reason why Anthony and Margaret had agreed to allow their daughter to move to Milwaukee; she would finally receive the education she deserved. The first year she spent exclusively studying reading and grammar at the Milwaukee College and by the end of the year, she was finally at senior high school level. The next two years, she studied math, keypunching, and various office equipment. When she graduated, she would be prepared for the new world of computers and corresponding office equipment.

This was the very first time she felt a sense of accomplishment and pride. Not only had she shed her fear of teachers sexually molesting her, but she finally learned how to learn and her frustrations melted away. For the very first time she was able to compete with her fellow classmates, which allowed her confidence to soar. With the interpreter at her side, she grasped her teachers' lessons and understood what was being taught. She was happy.

Carolyn became a pioneer for the deaf, as she was the very first student to bring an interpreter into a public classroom. Seated at the back of the room, the interpreter never interrupted the teacher except to clarify a question. As it turned out, it was a perfect symbiotic relationship; the school discovered a new tier of students who could be successful candidates at the technical school and the deaf students discovered a successful degree which allowed them to make a steady income. The fact that Carolyn opened doors to so many deaf students revealed a higher sense of purpose to her. Using her own success, she wanted to share that with others. This was the beginning of a new Carolyn, a fighter for the rights of the deaf.

One of her friends convinced her to go to a St. Patrick's Day dance. Although she couldn't hear the music, she could feel the beat and she knew how to dance. She had applied makeup, arranged her hair, and selected just the right dress, so when she strolled into the hall with her friend, heads turned in the pair's direction. Carolyn had no idea how beautiful she was; too many negative thoughts had cluttered her mind. James, dressed in a formidable tweed jacket, immediately walked over, offered his arm and escorted her to the dance floor. With her heels on, they were the same height. He stared into her dark eyes, brushed away his black hair and twirled her around the expansive dance floor. James was smitten. After several dances, he located a couple of seats in the back of the hall and they began conversing. In spite of her deafness, they communicated easily, he was patient and she attentive. When the band played the last song of the evening they walked out into the brisk March air, exchanged addresses and vowed to see each other again. James lived in Chicago, a mere ninety-mile difference, so the commute was doable. They made a date for the following weekend.

She couldn't wait for the weekend to arrive. Sharing a ride with several classmates, she rode to Chicago. Not only was she excited to see James, but she had never been to the city and was looking forward to the new experience. The moment she sprang from the car she felt a chill in the air and wished she had brought warmer clothing. Her friends dropped her off and they agreed to meet late Sunday afternoon for the return trip.

James waved, offered her a warm hug and walked her into the foyer of his mother's home. He had been forthcoming about Carolyn and his mother welcomed her with open arms. His father had passed away, so it was just the two of them living there. In spite of the darkness, Carolyn could surmise the neighborhood was upper class and she felt a bit intimidated. James was a perfect gentleman, showed her around the town, and took her to quaint restaurants, pubs, art exhibits, parks and stores. He held her hand tightly, hugged her shoulders, and gently kissed her, but never thrust himself upon her. He treated her with the utmost respect. He was falling in love.

Their relationship continued for many years as they alternated weekend commutes. He opened her eyes to the sophisticated culture of Chicago and she absorbed all that it offered. She observed and followed fashion, updating her clothing and makeup to city standards, refusing to look like a country bumpkin.

James held a steady and secure position at UPS. He loved his job and the fact that he could offer Carolyn a steady income if they should ever marry. Each day he steadfastly donned the ubiquitous brown uniform and performed his duties with care and precision. When he had to make a special delivery he was armed with dog bones to fend off any angry approach. It worked and he was never bitten. Once his father had passed away, he learned how to maintain the home and keep it in excellent working order. He became a proficient handyman making sure heat and hot water was always functioning and that the house was maintained. He saved rent living with his mother and saved up for a future he hoped to share with Carolyn.

A happy, normal life had finally arrived for Carolyn. Achieving success in the classroom and in her love life, she looked forward to each day. After three years at the vocational school, they handed her a diploma equivalent to a high school diploma. She moved out of her tiny apartment and found a larger place to live in Milwaukee. Walking around one of the smaller neighborhoods she noticed a 'For Rent' sign hung on a bakery. As she twisted the brass knob, the smell from the freshly baked bread wafted into her nose. When she pointed to the sign, the owner nodded her head and walked her up one flight to a lovely one-bedroom apartment. After a short tour of the kitchen, living room, and bathroom, the owner wrote down the price. At first Carolyn balked, exclaiming that no one wanted to live above a bakery and could she reduce the price? After some negotiating, they came to an agreement and Carolyn wrote out a check for the first month's rent. Walking around the spacious apartment, her creative juices began to churn. She would make this place her home. It would be a warm and cozy place to live, and when James would spend the night, he would feel the warmth as well. It would be their love nest when they were together. The only thing that bothered her was the constant sweet aroma from the bakery. *How would she ever keep in shape?* She responded by never indulging in the delicious stuff except on rare occasions when she would bring it to a friend's home for dinner. Slathered with butter, it was the best bread she ever ate.

After reviewing her intriguing résumé, Blue Cross, a health insurance company who had posted several data entry positions, offered her a starting position. Her first real job! She, along with a small army of data entry clerks, helped the insurance company grow. The business was a prime candidate for all the computer age could offer. Carolyn was there at the right moment. The advent of data entry allowed huge amounts of information to flow seamlessly in and out of hundreds of thousands of accounts. Her work was a needed commodity and it was the vocational rehabilitation school that assisted her in obtaining this position.

Opening her first bank account, she quickly learned how to handle money. She was cautious and spent sparingly; the day would come when her parents could no longer support her, and she had to plan for her future. James was a big part of that picture; she was very much in love and hoped he would pop the question and they would live in wedded bliss forever. For the moment, the couple continued to commute on the weekends, spending every minute with each other but never mentioning marriage.

Eventually the couple began to get intimate. Tarnished from her hellish past, Carolyn had never experienced pleasure when it came to love making. Always a gentleman,

James took it slowly and gently and their relationship reached a new level. Carolyn never shared her past as she feared it would either give James *carte blanche* to exploit her sexually, or worse, he would lose all respect for her and her parents. And although she enjoyed her first love affair, it was not without deep reservations. Incapable of resolving ten years of abuse, she often flinched when James reached to take her hand, or grabbed her arm. The simplest overture could put her mind in a tailspin. She tried to conceal her emotions but oftentimes the fear was written clearly on her face. Luckily, patience was James' middle name and he was always calm and gentle when it came to intimacy. He too pictured life with Carolyn and shared the eventual dream of marriage.

According to a psychological evaluation, Carolyn was, and still is, plagued by thoughts of abuse every day. At times she is unable to get those thoughts out of her mind. She had and still has constant dreams, nightmares and sleep issues which interfere with the daily task of living. The sexual abuse received at the hands of the nuns and priests never left her. Day and night she is constantly reminded of her past; sometimes it is a subtle remark, or a reminiscent smell, or a touch, but it is always lurking, waiting to disturb her train of thought. In spite of her accomplishments in school, work and love, her life was and still is hard to live. Every day is fraught with a struggle to fight the demons of the past and live sanely.

She stares at the screen shaking her head at the interpreter: no that's not right, that's not how I feel, that's not what I am thinking. The screen goes blank and a few minutes later another face appears.

"How can I help?"

After introducing herself, Carolyn tries again to explain what she is thinking and what she wants to say. This time the interpreter comes closer to matching her mindset. Sign language isn't perfect communication; yet no human communication is without flaws or lack of clarity.

Pressing her fingers to her forehead, she summons up the courage to talk about the nightmare that ravaged her sleep the night before. Living in a tiny community, there is no one to share her most inner thoughts with, so she plugs into the deaf website and signs. The communication is translated into an email and now, in black and white, her feelings are transcribed. It all sounds complicated and in fact it is but at least Carolyn has an outlet to express her reflections. So much is pent up in her mind, she feels compelled to transmit those feelings from mere thoughts to readable communication that can be shared with the world.

So many children, so many hurt minds and souls destroyed by St. Johns' clergy. No longer able to remain silent, she wants to tell her story. Surprisingly, after so many years, no one had dared go this route; no one had put down on paper what had happened at that school. A tear trickles down her cheek; perhaps it is all too painful to rehash the past, yet the reality is that she is reliving her past every day. Her mind is stubborn and refuses to allow her to forget. *What about the others? Did they forget?* Raising her eyes to the ceiling she shakes her head, *no, they didn't forget.* Returning her gaze back to the screen, she continues the story.

Chapter 9

After a fight with James, she opted to move back home and spend time with her parents. It wasn't easy returning home to Oshkosh; most of her life she had lived away from the family. There were so many lost experiences and so much hurt and guilt. The closeness with her parents had been severed the day Carolyn was dropped off at St. John's, and it was never recaptured. The bedroom she had once shared with her siblings had long since been abandoned. She had the room all to herself. Unlatching the beveled glass window, a gentle breeze washed through the room. The air was cool and crisp, a perfect late spring day. Setting her suitcase on the floor, she looked around; it was familiar but it now seemed lonely with her siblings were gone. She was the first to leave the home and now, in her early twenties, the only child returning, even if for one weekend. It was quiet and still, the traipsing vibrations of her siblings just a memory. Even though she couldn't hear, her other senses registered solitude. The flickering shadows as her brother and sisters galloped through the hallways were gone: everything was clean, unfettered, with no clothing strewn in the room. Sighing, she wished it wasn't all that peaceful; she would much rather be able to hug her siblings, talk about her life and share experiences. This moment instigated old bitter wounds of how much she had missed and with each passing day, as the still of the home became more persistent, the hurt dug deeper and deeper. A hurt too deep to ever patch together.

Carolyn felt a gentle tap on her shoulder, and twisting around she beamed when she glimpsed into her mother's face. They hugged and kissed and shed tears of joy. Her daughter was home for the weekend, and it was Margaret's opportunity to make up for so many lost years and so much

Carolyn's parents.

guilt. She would never be able to capture the hurt in her daughter's mind, all she could hope for was to ease the pain with an endless display of daily love. She couldn't undo so much pain, but she swore from that day forward she would try and make amends.

Margaret was proud that her daughter had completed her high school diploma and earned a vocational rehabilitation degree which earned her a decent paying position. When Carolyn announced Blue Cross had hired her, Anthony and Margaret were extremely proud. Margaret was keenly aware that she would not outlive her daughter and that plans and savings had to be put into place so Carolyn would have a bright and prosperous future. She prayed James would marry Carolyn and offer a stable marriage, but what if that didn't work out? She needed to help her daughter plan her future, but that was a conversation for another day. At that moment, all she wanted was to love her long lost daughter, to hold and squeeze her until all her love melted back into Carolyn's heart.

The parents spent the weekend doting on Carolyn and when Sunday afternoon quickly rolled around, she boarded the bus, returned to Milwaukee and began her new career at Blue Cross. A forerunner for employee's rights, they had no problem when it came to disability; there were other deaf and disabled employees on the payroll, and the company gave everyone a chance. She became exemplary, arriving each day on time, completing her work with a high degree of accuracy and managing to secure friends along the way. Carolyn truly appreciated the opportunity to work at a prestigious company and they in turn rewarded her with periodic raises. Each Friday when she returned to her cozy apartment she would wave her check proudly in the air and then deposit it securely into her checking account.

Frugal, she continued to spend as little as possible to get by but she also wanted to keep up with James's expectations so she made sure that she continued purchasing the latest in fashion and makeup. When she joined his mother in Chicago, she needed to show that she was aware of fashion and all that was new; it was just as important to impress his mom and she made the effort.

Because of the ninety-mile distance, Carolyn began branching out on her own. Independent, she sought out other deaf people who would eventually become fast friends. She went to basketball games and met a gaggle of deaf friends who gathered weekly during the season. They exchanged information, and soon Carolyn was an active member in the tight knit community. "We went bowling, to the movies, shopping, and did a lot of socializing. We would rent a small hall and have parties. It seemed as though every weekend there was a special event and we would all get together. We had endless parties and oftentimes we dressed up for the occasion. It became my hobby to sew beautiful dresses for these festive parties. I loved making the clothing almost as much as going to the parties."

Grooming was important, even at her job at Blue Cross. "If my hair got a little long, I would go and have it trimmed and styled and copy the way they did my hair. At the time it seemed very important to always look your best, from workplace to weekend, so I always made the effort."

Carolyn was living as complete a life as a young woman could. She craved the attention of her new group of deaf friends and they shared the same bonds. Finding deaf friends was a difficult task and once they were lucky enough to meet, they continued the relationships. Many went on to marry, have kids, and a few moved away, but there was a substantial core of friends to enhance and add great value to Carolyn's life.

It seemed as of late that the relationship with James was teetering on the edge; he was moody and oftentimes they fought. Putting all her eggs in one basket would be a recipe for disaster, so she continued to branch out and make new friends and develop relationships. One cool evening, she arrived at his home. The lights in the foyer were ablaze and he ran to grab her the moment he saw her shadow cross the front sidewalk. Picking her up in the air, he squeezed her tightly and kissed her ruby red lips. He removed her coat and offered her a small bouquet of flowers, then walked her slowly near the fireplace in the center of the living room. Not mincing words, he extracted a black velvet ring box from his pocket and asked Carolyn to marry him. Both shedding tears of joy they collapsed into each other's arms. Six years was a long time to wait for a wedding proposal. James' mother was privy to the event and proudly walked out of the kitchen carrying a bottle of champagne and three glasses. Toasting the couple, they all laughed that it was about time they made it official and planned a wedding. He had booked a reservation at a small family restaurant which would give his fiancé plenty of time to enjoy her new diamond ring. They celebrated their engagement.

Life was as good as it would ever be for the young couple, especially Carolyn. Over the six years, she and James could easily communicate and rejoiced in each other's company. They had come to know each other intimately and were ready to accept a life together. Carolyn could hardly wait to tell her parents and show off the engagement ring and then plan the big event. The couple spent the evening downing another bottle of champagne and eating a French gourmet meal. When they parted on Sunday, it was with great hesitation since it would be another week until they see each other. Returning to her small apartment above the bakery, she first called her parents and then began laying down plans for a modest wedding—she even planned on sewing her own dress. On rare nights, when she put her head onto her soft pillow the usual nightmares were replaced with wedding plans. Perhaps it was possible, even for one night to silence the demons.

Arriving at her work station on Monday morning she proudly showed off the engagement ring as her co-workers congratulated her. Even her boss was thrilled about the engagement. Despite her isolation from many workers, they all shared and rejoiced in her newfound happiness. And so her life went on, she working at Blue Cross and James working at UPS. The couple met each weekend and talked about their future, possible children, where they might live and the things they would do together.

Some months later, an odd turn of events occurred. As Carolyn emerged from the bus, she was greeted by James' scowling face. Alarmed, she grabbed his arm and they took seats on the closest bench. It seemed as though James had contracted a sexually transmitted disease and he blamed Carolyn for sleeping around, accusing her of causing his disease. Alarmed, she vehemently denied his allegations and promptly tossed the engagement ring on his lap. No matter how much she denied the fact she hadn't been unfaithful, he chose not to believe her. He knew she had a large coterie of deaf friends and he had convinced himself that one of the guys was responsible for her indiscretion. Carolyn shed tears, waited at the bus stop and took the next bus back to Milwaukee. That was the end of their six-year relationship, all brought to an end in a matter of moments. Crying all the way back home she vowed never to trust another man. Her heart was broken. All the plans they had made, the happy future, the hopes for a family, now gone. James never even gave her a chance to defend herself. He blamed the entire situation on her and never thought to look at who he was and the fact he had been unfaithful. "Years later he came to me and begged for forgiveness and asked to reconcile but I turned him down. I was so heartbroken I could never face him again." Her parents were sorely upset as was James' mother. The couple had come to an impasse and the marriage simply was not to be.

Sadly, she returned to her job that Monday morning with red eyes and without her engagement ring. Her co-workers guessed the marriage was off and offered condolences. This experience did not deter her from continuing to socialize with her deaf friends, but she never fell into another serious relationship. She had lost all hope of ever trusting another man. "It seemed as all the deaf men wanted to do is have sex with the deaf women and that was not on my mind. I kept them as friends but not as lovers."

Along with the break-up, the hellish dreams from life at St. John's reemerged. "I dreamed about the time Sister Renee kissed me too much on my mouth on a bus ride. I begged my mom to allow me to quit the school and mom said okay. Sister Renee told me it was time to go for lunch and I said 'no I want my mom.' I went to lunch and when I walked outside. I saw my mom at the bus stop. I ran as fast as I could to catch her but by the time I arrived the bus had closed its doors and taken my mom away. Sister Renee pulled my ears and tried to make me stop crying. I had been tricked and this time my own mother was part of the plan. I couldn't stop crying and I couldn't stop chasing after that bus."

That morning Carolyn woke up in a cold sweat, shaken from the dream. She had no way to cope with insurmountable abuse. So much to keep hidden and so much to process. The 'why' was never answered. Why did her parents allow her to go to St. John's? Why did they allow her to stay and why didn't they believe her rantings about sexual abuse? These questions would never be answered. This was her daily hell. Sometimes the memories were so ugly she was inconsolable. Her religion had failed her and she felt as if no one on this earth could possibly understand the cruelties she had suffered at the hands of the nuns. Raising up her hands to the sky, she prayed for help. *Someone please help me!*

Wresting with her pillow, the next evening she dreamed of the baths. How the nuns would strip her and bath her in front of several other nuns. They would insert their fingers into her private parts, spank her bottom, and fondle her chest, all due to sadistic pedophilia. She could feel the cool water running down her back and the tongues lapping at her genitals. They often left the door ajar so the priests could catch a glimpse of the Saturday ritual. The church had taken the most innocent, the most vulnerable and thrust their lives into the hands of the most evil of humankind. Sanity no longer existed, at least for Carolyn and the other innocent children. Not only did the clergy physically rape the child, but they left emotional scars that would never be forgotten.

There was no more wedding to plan, or rosy future to dream about. When her own doctor sent the results of her examination to James' doctor, proving that she had a clean bill of health, James refused to apologize. Their six-year relationship all boiled down to the fact he simply didn't trust her. But her life continued. She lived above the bakery, kept up her stellar job at Blue Cross and mingled often with the deaf community. She continued dating but was reticent to pursue a sexual relationship. She kept men at bay and dating encounters casual. She just didn't trust men for a myriad of reasons and was in no hurry to have her heart broken again. There were numerous divorced deaf men in her social group, and she avoided them. Divorce was not how she wanted her marriage to end. Although her own parents fought bitterly, it was apparent they loved each other and through the most difficult times they remained together. That was the kind of marriage Carolyn expected to have, a husband who would remain at her side no matter what.

Although James refused to apologize, it never stopped him from trying to restart the relationship. There were sporadic calls, flowers, gifts and notes, all of which Carolyn refused to acknowledge. It was she who would never trust him again. On any given weekend, she found numerous deaf men and women to socialize with, her life was filled with friendships and activity and for the moment that suited her just fine. Waking each morning, going to work, coming home to her own special apartment and later joining a group of friends, built her confidence and belief that in spite of her disability she could enjoy a fruitful, normal life. She had learned to succeed where so many others had failed, and, she had become a model citizen. With so many psychological obstacles in her way, Carolyn carved out a successful and meaningful life.

One thing Carolyn learned how to do was to speak up for herself. She wasn't afraid of asking for what she felt she was entitled to. She soon became an advocate for the deaf, helping others lead a fuller, richer life. Having a dog as a child, she realized they could be excellent companions, picking up on cues that the deaf are unable to notice. Because her other senses were, and still are, so sensitive, she observed her dog react to sounds. On Saturdays, when her Aunt would come to visit and the dog was in her bedroom, she watched his ears stand straight up and then he would race down the steps and stand at the front door. After months of observation, she realized that dogs could signal sounds and tell her when certain events were occurring. She carried those ideas in the back of her mind and would later implement them into a working concept to aid the deaf.

The September 1982 Sunday paper devoted a half-page to Carolyn, as she was one of the first beneficiaries of the Great Lakes Hearing Dog Program. Observant, she noticed that dogs display numerous non-audible behavior when there are important sound cues. A doorbell ringing or a siren while driving are salient sounds. Dogs can be trained to behave to these cues, alerting their deaf companion to pay attention. Through community sponsors, she was one of the first to receive a deaf-trained dog named Kim. The dog became an integral part of her life, going wherever she went and was one of the pioneer service dogs. The timing couldn't have been better. After she and James parted ways, the love and affection of a cute, devoted pet was a perfect solution. Kim was a constant companion, adding not only love but extending her ability to cope with the hearing world. In the dark winter months he would nudge her awake when he heard

Carolyn with her service dog.

the alarm sound, thus she was never late for work. When the phone rang he would jump up and run to the phone. She always petted and gave him treats in response to these behaviors. She was so thrilled with her new dog that she began spreading the word throughout the deaf community. She wanted everyone to be able to have this comfort and aid in their household. *The Hearing Aide News* ran two full pages of hearing dog placements made within the deaf community and she was pictured with her new dog.

In December 1982, the Sunday magazine *Insight* high-lighted an extensive article regarding the donation she received of a hearing trained dog. In the article entitled *Ears for the Deaf* it mentioned she was one of the first deaf persons to be given a hearing trained dog. She obtained the dog in Milwaukee and took it wherever she went, even her place of work. For the average individual, a dog is just a pet, but for Carolyn and the hearing impaired, the trained dog became an important part of enhancing and extending their lives.

After six years of keypunching at Blue Cross she began seeking alternative positions, but she was keenly aware that her grammar and writing skills were still lacking refinement. She had spent a great deal of time in Chicago and sought out Harper College, a new community college that accepted her application and promised to help her attain that goal. She had saved money and was prepared to put work on hiatus while she improved her skills. The enticement was that Harper College had on-staff teachers who signed: a perfect place to enhance her skills. She stayed a year and would have continued, but Margaret begged her to come home. The cry was so earnest that Carolyn felt compelled to return to Oshkosh. Her mother never mentioned that anything was wrong, only that she wanted her daughter by her side. At the end of the spring semester she said good-bye to her teachers and friends, boarded a bus and traveled home to Oshkosh. It had been a decade since she had spent any time in Oshkosh. Her friends were gone, so all she would have was her family, which for a young woman, now in her early thirties, would hardly suffice. She did what she knew in her heart was the right thing, her mother called and she answered.

Grabbing the metal handle, Margaret pried open the heavy oak front door and ran and hugged her daughter, shedding tears of joy as she kissed her. Standing back, she admired how Carolyn had grown into a sophisticated, beautiful and accomplished young woman. When Carolyn returned her mother's gaze, she was alarmed; her mother had aged well beyond her years. Clearly something was wrong and it became clearer why Margaret had asked Carolyn to return home. After tossing her luggage into her old room, she joined her mom in the kitchen. Margaret had poured two cups of tea and filled a plate with her famous cookies. Because Margaret was unable to sign, a pad and two pencils sat on the edge of the table as Margaret explained the problem. Although she had been a nurse, she had never taken proper care of herself and hated going to see the doctor. Anthony had spotted a mole on Margaret's back and she finally made the appointment. At first the doctor made little of the surface mole but during surgery things turned out for the worst; the cancer had spread over her entire body and there was no cure.

The couple had both quit their careers and opened a grocery store. Not only did Margaret need Carolyn's emotional support but Anthony needed help running the store. It was too much work for one person. Granted, the work wasn't glamorous—stocking, selling and maintaining the shelves— yet it was something Carolyn could dig into and be instantly successful. Carolyn adapted instantaneously, shedding her keypunching career for the life of a grocer and caregiver to her mother.

Between the grocery store and assisting her mom's needs, Carolyn's life was full and busy. Margaret was scared and so was Carolyn; neither knew what to do except to comfort each other, which meant a lot of hugging. One evening, Margaret motioned Carolyn to her bedside and handed her a piece of paper. The writing was so scribbled that it was almost impossible to discern; it read "I know, I know about the abuse and I never had the courage to tell you. Please forgive me for all that I have put you through." Carolyn looked up into her mom's eyes. She raised her arms, and wrapped them around Carolyn's neck. "I'm sorry, I'm sorry." They held each other until Margaret collapsed back onto the bed, sound asleep. Clutching the note Carolyn was at a loss; she didn't know how she should feel: sad, angry, glad, or filled with rage. Her mom knew all along. It just took the right moment and courage to admit she had prolonged her daughter's suffering.

With nothing but empty evenings, Margaret insisted that Carolyn restart her social life. "If I need anything, Anthony is here. Go, please and try to enjoy yourself. Have a little fun." Connecting with a deaf group, she began going to the socials. Someone would volunteer to be the host, select the venue and then notify the expanding group of friends. Carolyn had become an advocate for the deaf and did whatever she could to help the cause. She quickly developed a group of friends who shared not only their deaf disability, but a love for socializing and being active in the world. They hiked, skied, horse backed through rural areas, went to fairs, attended theaters equipped with captioning, and of course held dinner parties. She hosted a snowmobile party and over

300 people attended. "I love the snow and cold weather. This was a very successful outing and I made many new friends. It turned out that a lot of deaf people also love the winter months, the snow falling and the frigid temperatures as they are tactile experiences.

Carolyn became very close with many of the group members in Oshkosh except for one: Tom, who was in his early twenties. At one of the many socials, he introduced himself and his friend who was a teacher. For some reason, Carolyn discovered the teacher had no college degree nor credentials of any kind to be a teacher. Acting as an advocate, she drafted a petition and obtained twenty-five people to sign it. The teacher became incensed that anyone would question her credentials, let alone try to get her fired. Tom became extremely angry and supported the teacher. At the third social party Carolyn attended, Tom walked up to Carolyn and hit her on the shoulder, then repeatedly in the face. He threatened to kill her. All this was to protect the teacher. Grabbing her coat and purse she fled the party. A girlfriend grabbed her arm and the two left together. Crying, Carolyn was shocked at Tom's behavior. The two women returned to Carolyn's home and they talked for hours until Carolyn inserted the key in her newly purchased car and drove her friend home.

Worried that Tom would carry out his threat, the very next morning she contacted the police and had Tom served with a restraining order. The ordeal sent her mind in another tailspin as she vividly recalled St. John's where none of the teachers had degrees. The hitting on her shoulder and face opened the flood gates in her memory of the constant abuse suffered at the hands of the nuns. This time she became proactive. She would take charge of her life and she would never allow another person to hurt or intimidate her. That restraining order put Tom in his place and he never approached her again. As it turned out, he took a job at the post office and the teacher joined him. The petition served its purpose; unqualified teachers had no right to teach children.

During this time, Carolyn developed breathing problems. It could have been caused from several lifestyle issues; she began smoking, her stress level was escalating and the cold damp weather put a strain on her respiratory system. Unlike her mother, she didn't fear doctors and she made an appointment to see her physician. The doctor set up several tests and the prognosis was clear. She was diagnosed with asthma. The doctor prescribed several medications, breathing aides, strongly suggested she quit smoking and if possible, move to a drier environment. Although the symptoms eased, they did not completely dissipate.

After three short months, her mother passed away. The family was devastated: a mother so young to have died from a seemingly innocuous mole. Anthony called the doctor who pronounced her dead and Anthony and Carolyn began the draining task of funeral arrangements. Carolyn wrote cards and delivered them to Margaret's friends and colleagues and Anthony made the balance of the calls to the children and relatives. Tina, Margaret's sister, was hysterical with grief. She had always loved her sister, and now at such an early death she was overwhelmed. After the funeral was set, she planned the wake, which would take place at the family's home in Oshkosh. She arranged for the food and plenty of alcoholic beverages to be on hand and contacted the priest to preside over the funeral.

It was all so sudden. Anthony stood side-by-side with his children as he hovered over the burial plot. One by one they tossed a red rose onto the casket and Margaret disappeared from their lives. Carolyn callously tossed in a blood red rose. She felt nothing; she felt numb. Unlike her siblings, she shed no tears. "I was shocked when mom died. At the grave I realized I would never see her again, but my emotions were hidden. I felt nothing; no guilt, no deep pangs of sorrow. My heart was a blank canvas. For sure I knew I must have loved my mother, but in that moment, when my emotions should have become obvious, I never shed a tear. The time when children bond with their mother had been lost. I was sent away and for a decade had little contact with either parent. I loved them but I suppose the resentment of being sent away overtook all my feelings. Even in mom's death, I was unable to forgive her for banishing me from our home. Even though I understood they wanted what was best for me when I begged and pleaded for them to listen to the truth, they ignored me. It was my inability to forgive my mom that stopped up my tears."

Back at the house Tina made sure the preparations were in order and then spent most of her time with Carolyn, the one child she had doted over and tried to protect. Today, there was nothing she could do to ease the pain; they were all suffering. Nursing a glass of scotch didn't stop her heartache, it just calmed her nerves. There was such a large crowd, with people spilling out of the house onto the front and back porches. Hours later when the platters of food were as empty as the case of scotch, the crowd dispersed. All that remained were Anthony, his children and Tina and Nick.

It was not the right time to broach the question, but Carolyn had been called home to take care of her mother and now that Margaret, at the young age of 69, was gone, Tina worried about Carolyn's future. She was worried that she may lose her way. Finding a job was difficult with a disability. Every aspect of Carolyn's life had been a struggle, and now this devastating blow created another hardship.

That evening the children remained at the house, sleeping wherever there was an empty space. The next day they would all scatter back to their homes, but for one more night, they remained together mourning the loss of their mom. Margaret was filled with love and devotion to her children. Each child in their own way had made a success of their lives. She had prepared them to live honest and virtuous lives and, most importantly, she gave them the gift of love, which they in turn were able to share with their spouses and children. The only child lost in the nurturing process was Carolyn, locked away at St. John's. When Carolyn looked directly into her father's eyes, she wondered how many tears he shed over his wife. When Margaret admitted on her death bed she knew what was happening at St. John's, she knew that Anthony, too, must share in the blame. He had yet to apologize or admit the mistake; for the moment, his tears would align with Margaret. He loved her and prayed she forgave him for all his alcoholic rages. Neither of them had been equipped to properly care for Carolyn. No resolution was in sight. His answer was to drink and argue. He prayed Margaret would understand. They both sought answers in the Catholic Church, which turned out to be the nightmare that would destroy their daughter. When they searched for an answer or someone to blame, it could only be each other. A blame so deep that neither one of them could emotionally handle the guilt. Anthony's tears continued to fall as he thought about the love for his wife, the love for Carolyn, the endless mistakes, the drinking and the fighting.

Chapter 10

After the funeral, the siblings scattered back to their lives, but Carolyn was left alone in the house with Anthony. He soon returned to the grocery store, but she was at a loss. Her sole reason for returning home was gone and life appeared as a wide open abyss. She rewrote her résumé and began searching for a new job. In spite of her disability, between her education, prior job at Blue Cross and stellar personal recommendations, she would be a hot commodity. She just had to find the right position.

Anthony returned home from work and kissed his daughter. She had prepared a delicious meal and was proud she could bring a smile to her dad's face. Holding up the newly written résumé, she asked him to proofread it and make suggestions. The next day she edited the résumé and made a hundred copies. Still at a loss as to what to do or where to go, she picked up the local paper and the winter edition of the Hearing Aid News. An article describing a ski trip to Reno caught her eye. Reading every word, she discussed this with her father and made reservations the very next day. After so many bad memories, she welcomed a change of environment. Between St. John's, her mother's recent death and the threats from Tom, she needed to explore the world.

After purchasing some new ski gear and a few winter sweaters, at the last minute she placed several copies of her résumé into a waterproof plastic bag and packed it into her suitcase. One never knew when an opportunity might present itself. Kissing her dog Kim on his head, she promised to return soon, as it was only to be a short one-week vacation.

When she stood in line to board the plane, she noticed a few people using sign language. Apparently she wasn't the only deaf person going to the ski resort. Waving her ticket, she asked a gentleman if he would exchange seats, signing that she was deaf. He noticed the other woman was also signing and he generously gave up his seat. She was fortunate enough to sit next to a woman who was deaf. She worked in Reno and wasn't going to the resort. From the moment they buckled their seatbelts, they started a conversation that lasted the entire flight. Carolyn was truly happy: not only was she experiencing her first real vacation, but she had a buddy to tell her all about Reno and the amazing facilitates Lake Tahoe offered. Carolyn's eyes sparkled with delight as the woman signed about the great skiing and outdoor activities; it was truly a year-around resort.

As the plane banked, dropping its wheels in preparation for landing, Carolyn gazed out the window and was taken aback by the beauty of the majestic snow-covered mountains and the bustling city. She thanked her seatmate for her time and information, retrieved her luggage and boarded the designated bus to the resort. There wasn't an empty seat as 20 deaf people excitedly signed to each other about the trip, skiing and all of the activities promised in the brochure. The women were beautifully dressed and groomed for the cold temperatures, and were looking for a lot more than a breathtaking run along the slopes. This was an idyllic opportunity to find the perfect mate and with all the socials planned it was a strong possibility. But Carolyn was just seeking a great time in the outdoors and a few carefree days doing what she loved. Finding a lover or soulmate was the last thing on her mind.

The bus stopped abruptly in front of a rustic pine ski lodge. The husky driver slid open the door and unlocked the luggage compartment. Gathering their bags and equipment, the vacationers checked in at the front desk and were ushered up the wide carpeted steps to their rooms. Although the room was small, when Carolyn pushed back the curtains the sun's reflection on the snow illuminated the entire bedroom, making it appear spacious. Even before putting her clothing in the armoire, she anxiously read the activities and immediately set out for the slopes. There would be ample time later in the afternoon for emptying the stuffed suitcase. With a ski lift ticket in hand, she was prepared for the first run. Riding up the lift with another deaf woman, she felt exhilarated; the air was cool and dry, the sun bright and the snow pristine white. Gently sliding off the seat, she put a pole in each hand and followed the hundreds of skiers down the slopes. What an exhilarating feeling! Gliding over the powder, it was as if she had been skiing her entire life. Twisting and turning she was having the time of her life. No sooner had she completed a 20-minute run then she returned for another go. Putting both poles in her right hand, she took a seat and signed to the young guy seated next to her as the lift pulled them toward the top of the slope. He was there for the same reason, to enjoy a vacation with a group of deaf peers and was especially looking forward to all the social events. The men were seeking love interests just as much as the women.

With the onset of dusk, the lift closed for the afternoon and the die-hard skiers boarded the buses back to their respective hotels. It was dark when Carolyn returned to the lodge. Everyone was gathered in front of the oversized stone fireplace drinking a variety of alcoholic beverages and munching on appetizers. Although no words were spoken, there were plenty of smiles as the guests communicated with great animation; everyone was having a great time. Racing up to her room, she dropped her equipment in the corner, changed into a cashmere cream-colored sweater and black jeans, applied a layer of lipstick and joined the crowd. Not much of a drinker, she ordered a beer and slowly walked around the room seeking conversation. A young woman grabbed her by the arm and signed, "You look lost. How about some company?" They signed for a while, and she learned that the woman lived and worked in Reno. She told Carolyn the Veterans Administration was seeking employees. Carolyn's eyes lit up with joy; perhaps she would apply for one of the positions. Her new friend explained that even with a disability, jobs were available. She recalled that she had brought her résumé and perhaps she would take a chance and apply for a job. What could it hurt? The worst that could happen was that the employer would turn her down—but perhaps they would hire her. She spent the balance of the evening mingling with the house guests and later they boarded a bus which took them to a quaint rustic restaurant. A table had been prepared to accommodate all the house guests. The food was delicious and hearty, exactly what skiers sought at the end of a day on the slopes. That evening when she fell asleep, it was evident that the drier air had a positive effect on her asthma. Her breathing was calmer and she never had to reach for her inhaler. The doctor was right; that air was just what she needed.

The next morning Carolyn ran the early ski runs. When lunch time rolled around, she changed clothes and rode the bus to the Veterans Administration. Grasping her résumé tightly, she handed it to the receptionist along with a note that she was seeking employment. Smiling, the astute receptionist understood Carolyn's request and gave her a form to complete. Returning the completed form, Carolyn explained she had arrived in Reno for a vacation but would love the opportunity to live and work in the city. Later that afternoon she interviewed for a position. They explained that Carolyn could use an interpreter to assist her learning the position, that the VA was open-minded when it came to disabilities and happy to accommodate an excellent candidate if they required additional assistance. They would let her know.

She spent the rest of the week enjoying herself as she negotiated the slopes, interacted with new friends, and relaxed and unwound. The unfamiliar surroundings made her feel safe; no one there was a sexual molester and when men made advances a simple 'no' was all that was necessary. Finding a boyfriend was the last thing on her mind; she needed a change of scenery and Reno seemed to exceed all her expectations. To work in a city that offered year-around outdoor activities was exactly what she was looking for. The crisp cool air, the bright sunshine, the huge variety of sports, and a group of deaf friends answered all her needs. Reading the local paper, she researched housing prices. If she was offered a position she needed to make sure she could afford to live in Reno. She was pleasantly surprised by the housing prices. The more she researched the area the more plausible the move became.

On the last evening, there was an extensive cocktail hour and a lavish meal prepared for the vacationers. Mother Nature had cooperated the entire week, setting down a fresh layer of snow at night, giving the avid skiers perfect conditions. Dinner conversation was animated as they discussed returning for another grand week. Between the near perfect skiing and meeting a new group of friends, everyone seemed to have a truly wonderful time. Carolyn expressed her interest in returning; for her it would be a perfect place to put down roots. "Maybe some of you will join me," she signed.

Buckling her seatbelt, her feet felt the vibrations of the jet engines as the plane taxied down the runway and broke through the low lying clouds. On the flight home her seatmate didn't know sign language, but that didn't concern Carolyn since she had a lot to ponder. She was envisioning a rosy future and a good job. Reno would truly make her happy. But then her thoughts returned to her dad. She would be leaving him completely alone. Weighing guilt versus happiness, she rehashed her life and came to the conclusion that she had no guilt when it came to her parents; she felt that they had destroyed her life. She was resolutely working to create some semblance of sanity. Guilt for leaving her dad— absolutely not! For a solid decade he had ignored her tirades and her screams for help. It was her turn to do whatever she wanted to improve her life. Moving to a new town would twist the haunting memories deeper into her mind and allow fresher positive experiences to surface. Undoing the hideous ten years was impossible, but after her vacation in Reno there was a light at the end of the tunnel. Living a normal life was achievable.

Giving Anthony a perfunctory kiss on the cheek, she lumbered up the steps, tossed her gear on the floor, changed clothes, rambled back down the stairs and prepared dinner. Her dad sensed something was awry but didn't press. "How was your trip?" he signed, having learned a few common phrases to communicate with his daughter. Although tired from the long flight, she enthusiastically described the trip. Her hands were wildly flying as she described the slopes and the fantastic skiing. It was easy for her dad to see the jubilation in her eyes and the broad smile on her face. If only she could remain this joyful.

They sat down to dinner and after the dishes had been put away Carolyn joined her dad in the living room. Looking deeply into his eyes she explained that she had applied for a position at the VA and if they offered her the job she would be moving to Reno. At that moment she wasn't sure if she would be hired but she wanted to test the waters and let her father know she had every intention of leaving Oshkosh. He sat and listened intently and then hugged his daughter. He gave his approval for the move. As a parent he had been selfish and made far too many mistakes. If Carolyn wanted to move he would not stand in her way.

A few days later she received notice that she did in fact land the job. Ecstatic, she hurriedly packed her belongings, closed her bank account, and tuned up her car for the long drive west. Seated at the breakfast table, Anthony wished her well and then explained that he had been thinking about moving. Sick of the long cold damp winters, he was retiring to Florida. A couple old friends had enticed him into retirement and Florida was the perfect place to live out an easy, inexpensive life. He promised her that when the house was sold, she would receive a share which she could in turn use to purchase her own home.

With a packed car, two service dogs, and a set of directions she traversed the 1,600-mile drive in three days. The monotonous highway did nothing to dampen her spirits. Life would begin anew. Perhaps those nightmares would be buried in her psyche when blanketed with new experiences, new friends, a new job, and a new place to live. She hoped that changing everything in her current life would also remove the horrific memories of St. John's abuses. Running away from her past she thought she could also run away from recalling her childhood. The bright winter sun reflecting on the freshly fallen snow flooded the windshield. It felt warm, it felt comforting and most of all, it gave her a sense of safety. No one would ever hurt her again. In her early thirties, she grabbed the new opportunity with gusto. She wasn't seeking justice, just a chance to live a happy life. *Was that too much to ask?*

Pressing the accelerator to match the ascending road, Carolyn's view began changing. The thinner shorter trees were replaced with evergreens, and the low lying scrub was replaced by fuller, wider bushes. The trek through the mountains was filled with the beauty of the vegetation and the magnificent view of the snow-capped mountain ranges surrounding the city. Rolling down the window she inhaled a deep breath of the crisp dry air. It was invigorating. This new city, this new environment held the promise of an optimistic future. Glimpsing at the sleeping dogs huddled in the back seat, she smiled. Yes, even for the dogs it would be a better life. When Carolyn spied the road sign reading 'Old U.S. 395' she knew she had arrived. Slowly cruising down Plaza and Fourth streets, she turned the car north and began looking for a place to live that would take the two dogs. "There were many apartments to pick from. It was easy to find a nice, spacious, affordable apartment that welcomed dogs. That same day I arrived, I found a comfortable place to stay."

She didn't have to report to the VA facility until early Monday morning, which provided her enough time to investigate the city and surrounding area. Taking a test run, it was only a ten-minute drive from several apartment complexes to the entrance of the sprawling VA building. Driving around the building she noticed ample parking and wide windows covering a large portion of the exterior. *Must be plenty of natural light. I sure hope I get an office with a view.*

All seemed to be in order; it was time to find a perfect place to live. Driving back to the apartment complexes, she leashed the doggies and went for a long walk through the streets. Even though the temperature was below freezing, the rays from the sun were warmth enough. It all seemed peaceful: an easy place to live, with few cars traveling down the streets that were lined with apartments and homes. Of course on the weekends, the casino-packed downtown was wall-to-wall cars waiting in line to park in the lots. Reno seemed like the best of all worlds: a quiet place to live, but a few minutes away casinos offered a rich varied nightlife, and another few minutes away the mountains offered a multitude of outdoor activities. She knew this move was a great decision. She would focus on her job, making sure she would remain in this perfect environment forever.

On her walk through the center of the city she popped into a real estate office. Writing down her needs and the price she could afford, the office clerk handed Carolyn a list of options with directions. By noon, she had signed a lease, renting a spacious one-bedroom apartment. Although it was on the third floor with no elevator, that suited her just fine. The extra exercise would keep her and her dogs fit. Seated in the rental office, Carolyn wrote a check for the first month's rent and another for a security deposit. In turn, the manager handed her a copy of the rental agreement and two set of keys. She was home.

"I was really excited and happy to begin my new job. It was a chance to change my life for the better. I felt fortunate to have been given the opportunity to work at a great place." When one of the dogs nudged her awake on Monday morning, she sprang from the bed, showered, and dressed for her very first day on the job. After parking her car, she followed several employees into the building. Searching for the personnel office, a security guard pointed the direction. Mary Ann, an interpreter, introduced herself, gave Carolyn a tour of the facility and escorted her to her work area. To grasp the competency of the new employee, Mary Ann tested Carolyn's ability to keypunch and the results were more than required for the entry level position. Giving her instructions in sign language, a huge pile of work was set on Carolyn's desk, with a reassuring note that if she had any questions or concerns she should never be afraid to ask. "There is no such thing as a stupid question," signed Mary Ann. "We want you to be happy and stay here a long time."

With that Carolyn limbered up her cold fingertips and began keypunching a stream of data into the computer. After locating the bathroom, the supply closet and the water cooler, she was set in her new career at the VA. When the hour lunch break arrived, she again followed several employees into the cafeteria, munched on her brown bag lunch and scoured the room for other deaf employees but she did not find any. There were several employees in wheelchairs, and many with varying disabilities, yet she was the only one who was deaf. It turned out there were three other deaf employees but they worked the night shift and her only interactions were a short hello and goodbye. She wanted to make friends but from past experiences she knew it would be difficult; she would have to seek her social life outside the VA.

Monday through Friday, she diligently took a seat at her cubicle and entered data into the computer. Although the work was monotonous, she never lost sight of the fact she had a good stable job, lived in a fantastic city and had limitless opportunities on the horizon. Despite all the evil shrouding her childhood, she set it aside and concentrated on the good that life had to offer. Keypunching data eight hours a day, she was genuinely satisfied. The interpreter, Mary Ann, always answered her questions and kept her on track. Carolyn's work was satisfactory and her future secure. Suddenly, the competent interpreter was suddenly replaced by another one, who was unable to properly sign the directions. As the days melted into weeks, one of her supervisors became unhappy with her work, informing her that there were "too many errors." She began a personal crusade to oust Carolyn from her position. After relentless harping from the supervisor, Carolyn was demoted from data entry to housekeeping detail. Her job duties were drastically altered and replaced with mopping floors, cleaning bathrooms and dusting offices. She was devastated. Although she accepted the demotion, she immediately began seeking another job. This was not what she had spent years training to do. It was humiliating. Within six months she left the VA and began searching for another position.

Luckily Carolyn had always been conservative and had stashed away plenty of savings to sustain her until she found another job. "I had saved money and survived on my savings." During this jobless period she made the best of it by making new friends, socializing, enjoying the outdoors and improving her keypunching skills. The tight-knit deaf community was always sponsoring events; they needed each other and they needed to find spouses. Events of every kind were on the weekly calendar and included many venues, activities and creative interactions. Every deaf person was accepted. Deafness is a unique disability but when everyone in the group is deaf, it no longer becomes a hurdle; life is easier and comfortable.

Mary Ann, the interpreter who had assisted Carolyn at the VA, was extraordinarily upset with the dismissal and brought Carolyn to meet with an attorney who might rectify the situation. Carolyn didn't protest, but litigation was not in her blood. She accepted her fate, as she did all the other horrendous things that had come her way. The attorney appreciated and respected her feelings, and offered to help his client find another job rather than instigate a court battle. Reno is a small town and the empathetic lawyer had many friends. He was able to call in a few favors and his newest client had an interview with the US Army. There were numerous non-military positions and with Carolyn's skills, he was hopeful to find her a secure placement.

Herlong, California, seemed to be the perfect spot to live. It was but an hour away from Reno and the home of Sierra Army Base, soon to be Carolyn's new home. By any standard it is a tiny rural town, and about as remote as it gets. The majority of the population is a combination of a federal prison and the army base. It was as if Carolyn decided to banish herself from society and Herlong was an excellent hiding place from the rest of the world. Flat, dry, and sparse, the view from the only church in town was a vast open space. In a compelling letter from Lynn Pimental, she facilitated Carolyn obtaining a new job. Lynn was a friend of Mary Ann's and befriended Carolyn while she worked at the VA. Both Mary Ann and Lynn supported Carolyn by writing supportive yet pragmatic references. Lynn stated, "She is disabled on the basis of severe congenital deafness. Additionally, she has asthma. These disabilities limit her in the following manner: She is unable to hear oral instructions, communicate verbally, and must work in a clean environment. She is applying for employment as a supply clerk. Please accept Carolyn's application and consider her for the position."

Determined to land this job, she dressed for success, carried a few copies of her résumé and drove to the base. Unlike the sleepy town, the base was humming with people and activity, and didn't seem like a bad place to work. Seated on a hard oak chair, she nervously twitched while the personnel director read the résumé along with numerous references and Ms. Pimental's letter. Aware of the deafness, he knew the candidate would be able to perform numerous tasks. He didn't make her wait; she was hired on the spot. He opened his office door and ushered her into the adjoining office where she was handed paperwork, an employee's manual, and a description of the job. She would begin the following week. In October 1988, she began her lengthy career with the US Army.

Thrilled, she galloped to her car. It was a new job and a new opportunity. She would make this work. As she turned over the engine, she couldn't help but notice a layer of dust had accumulated on the windshield, and it had been less than four hours since she had parked the car. Taking another look around, she doubted if this would be the town she would live in—there had to be a better place.

Chapter 11

L ife in Oshkosh had changed drastically. Anthony moved to Florida and within a few years he passed away. The home he had promised to Carolyn was sold by her oldest sister who split the profits with Robert, her younger brother. Both went in different directions: Marie Ann to the north, and Robert out west to California. The family, once so close, had completely dispersed across the states. What hurt Carolyn the most was that the home promised to her by her parents was taken away by her siblings. What was promised and what was set in stone in the will were two different things. She lost out. Although she never counted on any inheritance, it was devastating when none came her way.

She faced the world on her own. With no family support, she had no choice. Luckily she was not only resourceful, but garnered support from others who admired and respected her ability to cope and conquer deafness.

The sky was a brilliant blue, the air clear, but the solitude and remoteness was too stark. Pulling into the only gas station in town, she grabbed a map from the newspaper rack and began searching nearby towns. Doyle, another tiny city fifteen minutes away, was her first stop. A bit more inviting with almost 1,000 inhabitants, more greenery, and several inexpensive apartments, it seemed like a better alternative to Herlong. The major issue would be the lack of a social life. Enjoying the interaction of other deaf friends would translate into a lot of driving. Life was finding the right balance and prioritizing; her job and making a living always came first. She had learned the hard way that family support would not be forthcoming. Elated with the job offer, she focused on the positive, filled the car up with gas and drove to Doyle. The short 20-minute drive was just far enough to alter the blank landscape of Herlong: with a variety of surrounding mountain ranges, at least there were picturesque views. Apartment living was cheap and so was raw land. Wisely, she chose to rent a modest apartment and if things went well with the new job, perhaps she would invest and purchase a piece of land.

Meeting the landlord, she scrutinized every inch of the space making sure it was clean, the plumbing was working, and there was no infestation of bugs. It seemed the only drawback was dust, everything she touched had a thin layer of high desert dirt. No place was perfect and if she had to pick a town to live in close to her job, Doyle was as good as it was going to get. Satisfied the building had been kept up, she wrote a check, collected a set of keys, drove back to Reno and commenced packing. She would miss the city and the majestic slopes surrounding Lake Tahoe, but making a living was her priority. With few personal possessions, she loaded up the car, secured the dogs in the back seat, turned in a northerly direction and drove to another new chapter in her life.

So far removed from Oshkosh and now Reno, she hoped the past would finally be buried. Nothing she saw, nor the people she met, or the new job, in any way reminded her of the past. Perhaps this move was the right choice. Despite the dust, her asthma symptoms had greatly diminished. She continued her love affair with the outdoors. Her two dogs always accompanied her on the long treks except when she opted for a bicycle ride.

For three years she kept a steady routine of work, socializing, exercising and peaceful contemplation. "I loved working with the military. The people were kind and I had a lot of friends. I looked forward to my job and took pride in the work." Although most of the work was data entry, there were numerous other tasks. When she needed to learn something new, she would read the instruction manual and if she had questions, an interpreter was made available to answer any questions or elaborate on details. Things were working out.

When payday arrived, she put most of the money in a savings account. She knew there would be rainy days ahead and having a nest egg would see her through tough times. Besides rent and purchasing food, there was little else to spend money on in the city of Doyle. Even if she wanted to, it would be nearly impossible to blow her entire paycheck in the country town that offered no entertainment and three restaurants. The few retail stores, while reasonably priced, did not offer attractive goods.

The winter holidays rolled around and she felt alone. "I never visited my older sister Marie Ann, who had moved to northern Ohio, nor Robert, who had moved out to California and become a real estate broker. I was so angry they had taken all the money from the sale of our parents' home and never gave me a share. I thought they were selfish." Pouting, she walked to the post office, slipped the key in the brass box and retrieved a letter from the Northern Nevada Center for Independent Living. It was written by Maureen Riccuiti, a Deaf Services coordinator whose employer offered advocacy support, referrals and relay (communication) services. They no longer offered interpreters since she moved from the state of Nevada to California. Rather, she would have the support of Nor Cal Center for the Deaf which would be able to offer interpreter assistance. Smiling, she folded the letter and placed it securely inside her leather satchel. At least she wasn't alone when it came to deafness; there were so many affected people that an agency had been set up specifically to make their lives richer and complete. No, she wasn't alone in her disability and that made her happy. She would make use of the services; any and all help was a welcome respite from despair.

Three years working for the Army had allowed her savings to swell to a comfortable amount. She began looking for a more permanent living situation. After purchasing a trailer, she spent the weekends trampling through raw land searching for the perfect view and the perfect price. "In 1989 I went to see a realtor to look for land for a house. I met William and he took me to look at properties. I asked him about the snow and if it was safe and he said it was. I told him I needed water, sewer and electric and William said he would help me. He even said he would get a man to shovel the snow for free."

Carolyn took her time scrutinizing the ten acres, walking in every direction, kicking the dirt, smelling the air and imagining the view. She memorized every curve, every hill, and was satisfied this was the right parcel to purchase. Although she had savings stashed in an account, she put down the absolute minimum payment and signed a mortgage. "When it came time to move, William helped me move the trailer to the property but when he stopped the truck on the property it was the wrong one. He insisted that this property was the best one for me. He then grabbed me and held me."

Her guard was down. What she'd hidden in her memory was beginning to repeat itself. She never gave a thought that this realtor would pounce upon her. She trusted him and naively believed that he cared about her when all he really wanted to do was swindle her and otherwise take advantage of her. To him, she was vulnerable, alone, and unable to scream out. No one would hear her cries. While William was trying to assault Carolyn, a construction worker was busy drilling for water. He opened numerous holes in the earth, yet no water bubbled to the surface. Exasperated, Carolyn kept protesting that this was not the property she purchased and that William should keep his hands to himself. After the construction worker jumped into his truck, foiled by the land, William continued pursuing his prey. "He begged me to kiss him and I said 'no' but that didn't stop him. He kept following me around the property. I was all alone, and no one could see him pursuing me." She fought, but he continued to wrestle with her. "I told him I had a problem with my vagina but that did not stop him." He threw her against the trailer and then to the ground. Hastily unzipping his pants, he held her arms and raped her. Then he rolled over, stood up, and pulled on his pants. He looked her in the eyes and thanked her and then lumbered to his truck as if nothing had happened.

Lying on the ground, stunned from the attack, she gathered enough energy to stand up. "I contacted Mary Ann, my friend and interpreter, explained what happened and pleaded for help." Mary was incensed and insisted on contacting the Doyle Police Department; something had to be done. Securing the dogs in the trailer, she drove into town. Carolyn spied Mary Ann seated on a bench as she walked into the small city building. Signing, she extracted as many details from the encounter as Carolyn was willing to tell. A few minutes later, the officer motioned them to sit as his desk. Mary Ann took over the conversation, explained the situation and then acted as a mediator between the officer and the victim. Carolyn refused to press charges; she wanted no part of a courtroom scene. Although this perturbed Mary, she was able to convince Carolyn to go to the hospital. Mary insisted on driving and after a four-hour wait in the emergency room, the doctors did a thorough examination. Not only did they concur she had been raped but her pubic bone had been broken, a sign that the attack had been rough. She made a decision: she would press charges and the local District Attorney of Quincy, California charged William with rape. Her wish was to keep this quiet; she didn't want this interfering with her job, but she knew at some time she would have to appear in court and face the accused.

The deputy district attorney mailed Herlong Army Depot a letter stating that Carolyn was under subpoena and would miss two days of work. The court assigned a translator, Karen, to assist Carolyn throughout the court hearings. The problem with Karen was that Carolyn didn't comprehend her signing; communication stagnated. Shortly after initial testimony, the district attorney dropped all charges and the judge dismissed the case. Carolyn was shocked by the decision, placing the blame on Karen's inability to properly testify. Her emotions ran rampant from anger, hurt, pain, humiliation, and finally depression. Was she never to have peace? She felt like a walking target, the entire world abusing her physically and emotionally. Observing a friend through these tribulations, Mary Ann knew she let her friend down. But the court selected the interpreter and she had to accept that. Mary Ann knew that had she been the one signing in the courtroom, William would have been found guilty. Life wasn't always fair and not everything was under one's control. True, Carolyn did not want to press charges, but when it came time for the truth, it was shrouded in a lack of accurate communication.

Against the police and Mary's advice, she remained on the property. There were two big problems: water and electricity. She easily solved the electrical problem by installing propane gas that generated more than enough energy for her needs. The water issue was resolved by purchasing buckets, filling them up with water and storing them outside the trailer. It was cumbersome, to say the least, but she was resourceful and determined to live on the ten-acre plot.

One day a letter arrived from her brother Robert. In it contained a contract with his sister offering to give her $30,000, her share of the sale of their parents' home. Flabbergasted, she readily accepted his generous offer. For Robert it was making amends; he wanted to be fair with his sister, a sister who needed family support. Robert drew up the papers and put them in the care of an attorney. The mortgage to her property was paid in full. Soon a letter arrived with the deed to the property. Although Robert's name was listed as the owner, it was in fact a gift. The parcel was ten acres perched on high desert allowing a spectacular panoramic view, the sun rising in the morning and the glorious western sunsets in the evening.

Building a house on the property would take more money than she was willing to spend, so she did the second best thing and continued living in the trailer. It was roomy enough and would serve her needs, which were simple. Maybe in the back of her mind the trailer offered mobility. If things didn't work out at the army job, she would always have a home, her own bed to sleep in, and a sense of security. Financially, she had no worries, as Robert had paid the mortgage off and her quarterly property taxes. She was left paying the utilities and upkeep on the trailer, which translated to less than if she were renting an apartment. The main drawback was the remoteness; she rarely saw people—just some animals scurrying in and out of the low lying bushes. There was no doubt the land appealed to her passion for the outdoors. Tall pine trees sprang up in clumps, interspersed with bushes, and huge rock formations bursting out of the sides of the hills.

Settling into the new location, she spent hours staring at the landscape; it gave her peace, solace and a sense of security. The sunrises were only matched by the sunsets, when the entire sky was lit with a rainbow of rays decorating the western edge of the earth. And for another three years she lived a quiet life. Working, meeting friends on the weekends and spending time with nature. Life was simple, unfettered and appeared sane. In fact it wasn't.

When darkness predictably arrived each evening, the nightmares of sexual abuse made their way to the surface. Flashbacks and spotty memories, interspersed with longer sexual scenarios took over her thoughts. It was rare when she had a string of nights of uninterrupted sleep. Within the darkness, she would thrash around the bed and then jolt upward, wide awake, shaking off the ugly memories of sexual abuse. She had run away and found a remote place to live, but those evil memories were never going to allow her the peace she deserved to have. *How long should I have to suffer? It doesn't seem fair that I can't shake the abuse, that my mind forces me to remember and I don't want to remember. I need to be free of these thoughts. What can I possibly do to change this? I moved far away, took a new job, live in a completely different home. Can I never run away from these torturous thoughts?*

Occasionally, on Saturday mornings, she would walk the dog (one dog had since died) to the only breakfast cafe in town and order a substantial breakfast. The food was simple but hearty and kept her full until lunchtime. Since Reno was a short drive, all her shopping was done in town. Filling up the empty trunk with essentials, including a large bag of dog food and a box of bones, she found all the items she needed and then she would make the short drive home. Reno became her only social outlet; it was the only place where she could socialize with deaf friends and although at times it was inconvenient, that was where she spent her weekends. When the snow fell, she waited until the highway had been cleared and then jumped into her car anticipating a wonderful day.

Life continued on; working for the army and returning home to take care of her pet and herself. She never thought about the rape. In fact no one ever came around; the ten acres provided a secure boundary. Other than a few unfriendly snakes, no one bothered her and the closest neighbor lived five miles down the road. Her mind rarely wandered back to the rape or the courtroom scene where he was pronounced not guilty She knew he would never bother her again. True, she lost the case, but she wanted him to know he couldn't take advantage of her and walk away without any consequences. She flexed her muscles and used all the law would allow to make him pay. He got off, but there was a trial and his name was tainted, his life and actions were scrutinized by the prosecutor and would forever be a part of public records. He didn't walk away unscathed and for Carolyn that was enough. So she never worried he would return.

Robert, her brother, was thriving in California working as a realtor. The brother and sister rarely saw each other but when she received word of his death, she was devastated. At 50, he had a massive heart attack and died. The siblings were shocked as were his wife and children.

Returning home from work, Carolyn grabbed a letter attached to the front door of the mobile home. Ripping open the envelope she was angry when it read the property was being foreclosed. Later there was a knock on the door and papers were served to vacate the property within thirty days. That didn't make any sense; Robert had given her the property with no strings attached. It was in fact her share of their parents' home. After making a series of desperate calls she discovered the truth. Robert had purchased the land, in his name, and contracted with an attorney to pay a mortgage each month. Upon her brother's sudden death, the payments stopped and the bank took back the property. She trusted her brother and knew nothing about this contract with the attorney. After six years her property was instantly taken away and she had no legal option. Angry, she sought legal advice, but it was too late. She had to vacate.

The next day at work her friends learned of Carolyn's dire situation. One of her neighbors stepped in and offered to allow her to park her mobile home at the edge of their 600-acre property. Situated up at the very edge of the parcel, they would hardly notice she was there. Thrilled, Carolyn hitched up the home, moved down the road and remained there for eight years. Her privacy and safety remained intact: no strangers wandered around and she was completely co-cooned on another remote piece of land.

When she should have been mourning Robert's death, all she felt was anger; he had withheld the truth through a secret contract with his attorney and now she was the one paying for his unexpected death. Like all of us, he never considered he would die, especially before his older sister. He thought he was invincible, at least until old age, and as far as he was concerned the contract would always be in place and keep his sister secure.

The sun   began to dip into the western sky as she sat on the edge of the bed pondering her bad luck. Forcing her mind to count her blessings, she scanned the trailer and it was hard to find any positive notes in her life. At least with the backing of a good friend she had a free place to stay until she figured things out. There was no more lugging bottles of water or purchasing propane gas; her friend hooked her up to the utilities and once a month she wrote a check.

Was deafness such a curse that it caused the world to treat me so badly? Had the world abandoned me? Certainly my family had. I thought brothers and sisters should support and love each other. What did I do to make them ignore me and worse yet, take away the one legacy left by my parents? Why is my life so hard? Can I never get a break?

The sky had morphed into rose tones, and then darkness arrived. The shimmering stars opened the heavens but could do nothing to provide hope to her waning heart. The love she needed wasn't available. Her mind was forced into dredging up enough strength to carry on and to deal with the demons that inhabited her mind. Staring at the cloudless sky, she summoned the courage to go on, focusing her thoughts in a positive direction. No doubt so much had been taken away from her, yet, only in her mid-thirties, life could offer her so much more. Staying strong and visualizing positive experiences was what made her happy. That was where the road should be traveled, and that was where she needed to be.

Chapter 12

Mary Ann was blessed with a quiet inner beauty that imbued both her body and spirit. Tall, with wide deep-set azure blue eyes, brown straight hair grazing the bottom of her chin, and an athletic figure, she was as beautiful on the outside as the inside. After befriending Carolyn in Reno, their relationship lasted for decades. She was an expert interpreter who came to have an intimate understanding of Carolyn, adept at comprehending not only the obvious but the subtlest of thoughts that lay below the surface. An advocate, Mary Ann clung to Carolyn's side and vowed to share the journey, wherever it might take them. She was the initial interpreter at the army base and remained by Carolyn's side throughout the rape trial, maintaining their relationship through good and bad times. MaryAnn became the person Carolyn could trust and count on, but she remained in Reno while Carolyn picked up stakes and moved to California. There were numerous times when they connected; she always made herself available to help Carolyn. A life so fraught with problems deserved to have a constant friend at her side. That was who Mary Ann became: not only a friend, but also an advocate. If there were battles to fight she would gallop in on a steed, pull out her trusty sword and lunge forward. No, she would never leave Carolyn behind.

Carolyn developed other close relationships while working at the army base. Sonny was one of her staunch supporters. Tall, dark and handsome, his appearance caught one's attention when he walked into a room. His military career was highly decorated. He was a brave and honorable man. He befriended Carolyn not only for her personality but also because he sensed she needed extra support; it was tough going through life with a disability. As the years progressed and Carolyn's boss began to nitpick her work, he was the one who stood up for her. "He supported me and if there were problems he would always be on my side. He helped me get interpreters who I could communicate with and arranged a meeting with the translators every two weeks for over seven years. That was a great friend."

Sonny was sensitive to her needs. He had never interacted with deaf friends or acquaintances, yet he seemed to anticipate Carolyn's needs and willingly secured her future by providing a fluent communicator. Observing her work and demeanor, he was proud to be part of her life. As a black man, he suffered the sting of prejudice and if he could redirect those feelings towards helping another human being, he would make the effort.

She looked up from the keyboard and saw Sonny's wide smile. That was all she needed for encouragement, and that was all she needed to make it through the day. Another moment later she glanced at the bottom of the computer screen. The clock read 5:00, time to log off and make the half-hour drove home. As she emerged from the brick building, a brisk northern wind caught her coat and tiny drops of snowflakes tickled her face; it was going to be an arduous drive. Turning off the main road the car crawled a quarter mile on the gravel to the trailer. Once home, her dog galloped out the front door, running into the bushes. He was undaunted by the frigid temperatures. Hanging her coat in the closet, she was thankful that she no longer had to lug propane tanks; the trusty electrical poles stood a couple hundred yards away and provided all the energy she needed to live comfortably. It would be a quiet evening; she would not be venturing out into the snowstorm. The trailer was stocked with provisions, so neither she nor the dog would want for anything. Self-reliance had become second nature. Wise and frugal with money, she always anticipated needs. Living in the high desert for almost a decade had taught her how to survive the worst of circumstances. That day was just another instance where her knowledge of the surroundings assured her survival.

Luckily when Friday rolled around a strong westerly wind had blown the storm eastward, the roads were clear and she was on her way to Reno for a night of socializing with her deaf friends. The single men found her attractive and vied for her attention. Flattered by the attention, Carolyn became immersed in numerous conversations, but when it came time to go home, she climbed into her car and drove home alone. With so many raw memories of sexual abuse, she had sworn off men forever, at least in a sexual way. The rape was the last incidence she could possibly endure. From her perspective, all men sought only one thing when it came to women and that was sex. "They would sometimes taunt me and call me gay. No one knew my life and I wasn't about to share it." She kept the men at bay, and after a while, they finally accepted the fact that no one would be taking her to bed.

The deaf group met at a bar inside one of the casinos, drank a few beers, ordered burgers and later congregated at the bowling alley and played until midnight. When they finally said goodnight, one of the women signed that another social was planned for Saturday; they would meet at the slopes in the morning, spend the day skiing, and meet for drinks and an early dinner. On the dark drive home, Carolyn was anticipating another great day shared with friends, and enjoying her favorite sport. She was happy, content and satisfied with life. For all the evil that had come her way, she was experiencing a love for living. Between the 40 hours spent in the tiny township of Doyle, socializing and playing with her dog, her life was rich and full. She took care of her health, both physical and mental, settling into a calm routine. She made an effort to push away feeling sorry for herself, rising each day determined to make the best of the life she was given.

Saturday morning she dressed for a day on the slopes and brought a change of clothing for the late afternoon activities. She also brought a large bag stuffed with dirty laundry. Living in a trailer does have some drawbacks and room for a washer and dryer was a luxury she didn't possess. Each

Saturday, regardless of the social plans, one hour had to be set aside to wash and dry her laundry. It wasn't so bad and oftentimes she would meet people. The laundromat sat on a lonely corner on the outskirts of town surrounded by several old apartment buildings, and there was no place to change a dollar bill. "This challenge was easy; I must admit I love to gamble and there were plenty of places to do that in Reno. My favorite game was bingo, but I really enjoyed playing the slots. I have always been very careful with my money and gambling was my only vice. I set a limit and if I lost, I walked away, but I always made sure I had plenty of coins to do my weekly laundry. Gambling served two purposes, giving me enjoyment and insuring my clothes got clean."

After several runs on the slopes, she met a couple of friends in the lodge for lunch and then returned to the slopes until the last ride up the mountain for the afternoon. The resort was packed with skiers and she was careful negotiating through the powered snow; she didn't want to get hurt as she needed both legs to get to her job. Finishing the last run she removed her skis, drove down the plowed road and pulled into a bar where a bunch of friends were meeting. Grabbing the small bag holding a change of clothing and stylish shoes, she ducked into the bathroom, dressed, applied makeup and brushed out her hair. Looking in the mirror she observed several other women and realized that she appeared no different; in fact, she felt prettier and in better shape than most. Walking out of the busy bathroom, she felt like one of the crowd. No one would notice she was deaf and this scenario made her happy. She dressed, walked, and smiled as any other girl would. At that moment, being deaf didn't feel like a disability and with the music banging in the background, conversations were almost impossible.

Waving to a couple of friends, she took a seat at the reserved table and began signing. They realized conversation was flowing easier at their table then at the rest of the bar. One couple got up to dance, but Carolyn refused, preferring to remain at the table catching up on stories of skiing. She loved learning about the best run, the driest snow and the least crowded slopes. The waitress took their orders and they spent hours munching on bar food and drinking tall glasses of home-brewed beers. Yawning, she looked at the large round face on her watch; midnight had struck. It was late and she had a half-hour drive home and the dog needed attention. Saying good night, she gathered her bag filled with wet clothing and walked into the bitter cold air. Maneuvering through the pitch black curvy road, she was already anticipating the following weekend. Plans had already been set, she had a lot to look forward to.

Sunday was never a day Carolyn spent in church—that tradition was relinquished when the clergy at St. John's ignored their bibles—but it was a day of rest. There was never a plan; she devoted the day to relaxing, keeping healthy and playing with her dog. A long hike was always in order unless the weather was too severe. She would walk for miles, taking alternate paths each weekend. Exploring the trails was exciting, as there was always something new to see and animals were abundant; wild horses, donkeys and deer of all sizes roamed nearby. Sometimes the dog would bark, but she didn't hear him, then as if out of nowhere, a large deer with wide antlers would cross their path or a pack of horses would come running through the taller grasses. She kept her eyes wide open for those incredible experiences. Mother Nature filled the earth with life and wonderment; living in the mountains provided a front row seat to all this beauty.

The two-hour trek was exhausting for the dog as she observed his tongue hanging out the corners of his mouth. Gulping down some water she splashed some water into his mouth, turned around and headed home. That night, like on most Sunday nights, the house was quiet, the dog slept like a log the entire night. Even when she clapped her hands he didn't stir.

Walking in the wide open spaces was a stark contrast to her working conditions. Her workspace was a tiny compact cubicle and at times she felt stifled, as if she couldn't breathe. The weekends gave her eyes a chance to see beyond the two-foot space and her mind a chance to inhale fresh air.

She rarely allowed the lack of space to bother her as she was always so busy but sometimes when a fat pile of documents arrived and there was no room except to place them at her feet, she felt pangs of claustrophobia.

It crept up slowly, so subtly that Carolyn was unable to read the signs. Tommy, one of her superiors, began harassing her about job performance. He then convinced three other employees to join him in ousting the deaf employee: Sherrie, Steve and Roy. It was 1989 when Carol Beach, director of the facility, called a meeting between Carolyn, Sally, her boss Myrna, and the army-provided interpreter Mary Ann. Carol took charge of the meeting as Mary Ann communicated the proceedings to Carolyn. There was a pall in the air as the room took on a chilly feeling; a stack of papers was dropped in the middle of the metal table. Pointing to the pile, Carol turned and looked directly into Carolyn's eyes, "Those are your mistakes," she announced. "Too many. Unacceptable!" Turning to Myrna, she insisted the interpreter come to the office weekly to make sure Carolyn was on track and understood her job duties.

Myrna was angry; in the past there had been a few deaf workers under her tutelage and none of them had ever requested interpreter assistance. The director explained that federal law specifically stated deaf workers had a right to such outside services. The EEOC (Equal Employment Opportunity Commission) protected workers from discrimination. Carol intended to hold Myrna's feet to the fire, and demanded she allow Carolyn access to an interpreter. Not only was it the right thing to do, but it was a federal law.

In June 1990, a cryptic one-page Initial Interview Data Sheet was entered to the EEOC by Carolyn as evidence of discrimination. It read: "I feel I have been discriminated against based on the following; no interpreter was made available during meetings." According to the law, she had every right to obtain assistance during important meetings, but was denied that right. Unable to know what was said, she never learned whether anything said would affect her job. If a written document had been provided perhaps this entire scene might have been avoided. Even in the brevity of a short meeting, the director of such a meeting had the duty to communicate with everyone; but in Carolyn's case, the director simply forgot the needs of this employee.

On July 31, 1990, Carolyn's prayers were answered. The Department of the Army prepared a memorandum for a Negotiated Settlement Agreement dictated by Orlo Roy Jensen, Director of Logistics. "In the interest of promoting its Equal Employment Opportunity Program and to avoid protracted litigation, the Army agrees to settle the complaint. The Army does not admit that it has violated Title VII of the Civil Rights Act, and agrees to the following: eighteen hours of training. The additional training will be provided by the Supply System Analyst and Division Chief for the Directorate of Logistics. The training must be accomplished with thirty-five working days of the final signed agreement. Training will be documented as 'on the job.' Management has provided a pamphlet 'People with Disabilities.' The intent is to provide to the immediate co-workers information in relation to possible individual misconceptions that could arise in dealing with people with disabilities."

The settlement demanded Carolyn sign her name and once signed, her rights to sue were waived. No attorney was privy or witnessed this action. But a disclaimer was added stating that if she believed the Army had failed to comply with the terms of the settlement, another office could be enlisted to ensure the settlement's terms were met. Carolyn signed on the dotted line, hopeful that she would be treated fairly and in accordance with the two-page document. She shook Mr. Jenson's hand and walked away, confident her rights would be honored. He simply offered a perfunctory nod, as if to acknowledge they were all in accord. Returning to her cubicle, she turned on the computer, entered her password, grabbed a stack of invoices and began keypunching away. Her job was safe, at least for the moment, and she was happy and secure. Thinking back on the agreement, she wondered if forcing her co-workers to read and abide by the EEOC rules would create a sense of resentment and perhaps cause her to lose friends, or destroy long-term relationships.

Shrugging her shoulders, she began keypunching away. Focus was paramount as she had to continue proving she was capable of handling the work. Sally Pain had acted as her representative during the proceedings with Mr. Jenson and Carolyn was confident that all went well; there was no need to worry; her situation was secure. A couple of days later a memorandum was lying on her desk. The subject stated "Disqualification of Complainant's Representative." Sally Pain was disqualified from representing Carolyn in the complaint. Craig Christensen, who had reviewed the file, stated that Sally had a "conflict of interest due to her duties as Directorate of Logistics." Carolyn set the one-page document down and began to shake.

What does all this mean? The settlement? Does this mean it no longer is in effect? Who do I turn to? Who is going to help me? Why is my life so hard? Every step forward seems to bring me further from away from resolution. The woman I counted on to help me doesn't count! Seated in her cubicle, she screamed, but no one would hear her cries.

Harassment came disguised in many forms and so another memorandum was set on Carolyn's desk. The author, Tammie Dunn, Chief Property Branch, complained of an unapproved absence. Tammie oversaw Carolyn and did everything in her power to oust the employee. Tammie, as supervisor, complained about Carolyn's absence. She held the reins and if her employee was to attend a meeting or appointment it first had to be cleared by her, regardless of the situation. To further antagonize Carolyn, Tammie noted that on August 20, 1991, Carolyn failed to notify her of a mandatory meeting she was attending, even though it was Tammie herself who had scheduled the meeting. The supervisor complained that Carolyn did not notify her regarding the topic or time of the meeting, and that she left the work site without prior knowledge or approval. The supervisor purported that it was Carolyn's responsibility to notify her of any scheduled meetings and failure to do so would result in an unfavorable action such as being placed on absence without leave. That Tammie complained about a meeting she was responsible for setting and blaming Carolyn for not telling her about the meeting was farcical. It was her own job that could be placed on the chopping block if the EEOC elected to find her actions as discriminatory. That derogatory note would unnerve Carolyn and, Tammie hoped, cover her own ass.

Sally Pain was also the recipient of the same memo. Two months later, she filed a formal one-page charge against Sierra Army Depot. Compelled to defend Carolyn she wrote the following: "Since on or about October 1, 1991, the above-named activity by its supervisors, has failed to provide the exclusive representative with data requested by the union concerning equity in work load on computers in this case." Terms detailed in the settlement had been ignored. Proof that Carolyn's work had been sub-standard had not been provided. Supervisors who wanted to oust her from the job had done nothing to state their case which all boiled down to one simple word: discrimination. Even though Sally was disqualified she could still file charges against the army base. When Carolyn read through the simple statement she felt elated that Sally was still leading the charge, yet worry plagued her mind. *Was this going to be enough? Will on-the-job harassment ever cease?*

Now in her sixth year on the job, after establishing a routine, aligning friendships and building a stable life, it was all hanging in limbo. The demons fomenting in her psyche broke through to the surface and stole her sleep at night. Nightmares of St. John's sexual abuse became intertwined with the harassment of her job. The world was collapsing around her and it seemed like there was no way to stop the train wreck. She could only cope with so much pain. She needed help. In the middle of a night, sweat poured from her brow, her heart raced and her hands trembled. Padding to the window, she thrust open the glass, held her arms toward heaven and begged for help. She felt vulnerable as if the very core of her being was unravelling. It was the job that held her life together, that provided purpose, sustenance, human interaction, and mental stimulation. If that was gone her life would become an empty void. She couldn't allow that to happen. She had to fight.

And fight she did. On December 10, 1991, the Office of Equal Employment Opportunity, Department of the Army sent a formal notice of receipt of a discrimination complaint filed by Ms. Carolyn. It acknowledged receipt of the filed complaint and provided her with notice of the rights and the time requirement for exercising those rights: "If your complaint is accepted, it will be investigated. Based on the information developed by the investigation, an attempt will be made to resolve your complaint informally. If your complaint is rejected, the rejection will be considered a final Army decision on the complaint. You will be advised at that time of your rights of appeal. If an informal settlement is not reached, you will be notified in writing of the proposed disposition of the complaint. You will also be notified of your right to request a hearing by an administration judge who will recommend a decision to the Army. Instead of an appeal to the EEOC you may file a civil action in the proper U.S. District Court."

After carefully reading the letter, it was clear that the Army was aware of the discrimination complaint and was willing to state in writing all her rights. Never did the Army admit any wrong doing; their response was simply to ensure that all her legal rights and alternatives were precisely spelled out. Breathing a sigh of relief, she was thankful for the acknowledgement of the complaint and the fact they were willing to try to listen to her version of on-the-job harassment and prejudice.

Folding the letter, she slipped it into her purse, waiting patiently for the next step. It came two days later in a letter written by Craig Christansen, Equal Employment Manger. "Based on my review of your complaint and discussion in my office the issues accepted are as follows: not receiving a promotion, not receiving adequate training and not allowing an interpreter of your choice. Your complaint will be assigned to an investigator for formal investigation."

She breathed another sigh of relief; the Army accepted a portion of her complaint and was willing to allow her the opportunity to expose the unfair acts visited upon her as an employee of the Army. She would have her day in court. She could never undo the harassment she endured from supervisors and managers, but at least they would be officially charged with prejudicial conduct.

Chapter 13

The approaching winter holiday season was cloaked with despair. The complaint weighed heavily on Carolyn's mind and no matter what she did it was all she thought about. At weekend social events she often brought up the subject but none of her peers had ever experienced the situation. Granted the deaf had endless problems but no one had felt the brunt of bias as Carolyn did. Offering condolences and general advice, her friends encouraged her to continue fighting. A few bad supervisors shouldn't take away her rights. Hugging several friends, she thanked them for giving her the courage to pursue the complaint. "The Army is willing to supply me with an attorney if I couldn't afford one and I may take them up on that offer. With my job on the line, I could hardly afford any additional expenses. That offer may just prove the Army knows I have not been treated fairly and all those petty remarks are just that, petty remarks by nasty people."

Grabbing her ski parka, she waved to her friends and walked briskly to her car. A bitter northern wind had blown the snow clouds away revealing a sky blanketed with shimmering stars. The cold air was invigorating. Strength of will replaced hopelessness. She wasn't alone in her battle with the Army; friends, attorneys, and advocates were going to see her through the raging storm. This time her battle was transparent; everyone could see the harassment. This was different than the decade of frustration when the clergy of St. John's waged their sexual war against her and she suffered alone. This time she was flanked by a battalion of caring people invested in her success. She had done her job, showed up consistently and reliably for six years, methodically delivered the work. She would defend her career; she would make them all understand that deafness didn't mean she or anyone else was stupid or inferior. It meant that communication was a work in progress Her supervisors were incapable, or lazy, or uncaring about her life; they wanted it easy. They didn't want to be bothered with an employee who required extra assistance.

After Carolyn unlocked her trailer door, the dog scrambled outside and then quickly returned to the warm cozy home. Carolyn added some water and food to his dishes, took a quick hot shower and slithered underneath the warm covers. Turning on the small television, her eyes adjusted to closed captioning and she eventually fell asleep to the local news. It was a refreshing change; she had a peaceful night as she dreamed about the bustling bar, her friends and the solace of another weekend ahead. Several feet of freshly fallen snow had covered the mountains, she would definitely be on the slopes.

Notice came to her dated February 5, 1992, a month into the new year. It was from the Department of the Army, Office of Equal Opportunity, the subject of which was a notification of a formal investigation to be conducted on her discrimination complaint. "You must notify us in writing if you want witnesses on your behalf. You need to tell us what information they can contribute to the case." The hearing date was set for the following month. Carefully reading the notification several times, her mind mulled over prospective witnesses; but would they testify on her behalf? She didn't have the answer. Her co-workers were loyal, yet testifying might place their own jobs at risk or lead to future harassment. She had a lot of thinking to do.

Two days later, Carolyn was copied on a memorandum sent to the commander of the Sierra Army Depot, the individual with the highest authority, from Angel Martinez, Investigator. In it, Mr. Martinez explained that he had been assigned to investigate the complaint and this document would serve as official notice. The defendants were noticed to commence preparing for the preconference hearing scheduled in March. The purpose of the conference was to clarify the procedures to be implemented, clarify the basis of the complaint and to review if any attempts have been made at resolution. A court reporter was to be hired for two days to record the proceedings. Tammie Dunn, Carolyn's supervisor, would be required to respond to the allegations as set forth in the complaint and she would be required to testify as a witness. All discovery was given a cut-off date and was to be submitted in triplicate. Additionally, a guide was enclosed which provided a lengthy detailed explanation of what was expected from all the participants.

Mr. Martinez had covered all the bases, properly notified the subjects of the complaint and sent a copy to the plaintiff. It was up to both parties to review the guidelines and re-spond according to the basic rules of discovery. This was not an easy task for Carolyn since she was unable to afford an attorney, but then she remembered one would be provided. Clinging to the memorandum, she slid it into her purse—yet another notice to add to the growing pile of litigation docu-ments. It was impossible for her to figure out if this notice was positive or negative regarding her case. All she could do was read it and place it in safe keeping. The hearing was a month away. She wished she had a deaf friend who was an attorney; that would make her life so much easier, but she lived in a tiny town with limited options and no such attor-ney appeared on the horizon.

Carolyn completed an Occupational Disease report where she listed in detail the harassment from Tammie Dunn, her supervisor. "Due to the proposed suspension and insubordination (as proposed by Ms. Dunn), I have been up-tight, can't sleep, nerves are bad. I get upset really easy. This harassment has been an on-going event over the years. She gave me a reprimand and a threat for removal charging me with AWOL. The harassment continued; she wanted to give me time off but with no pay." (With six years on the job, Carolyn had earned a hefty amount of personal time off).

Ms. Dunn harbored prejudices and continually agitated the employee at her whim. Perhaps the supervisor lacked compassion, or complete ignorance when it came to interacting with the deaf. She was determined to make Carolyn's work life hell, and the harassment continued with threats and admonishments. What was in the supervisor's mind that made her so mean? And why did this behavior continue for so long? What was she afraid of?

For a while things at the job seemed to settle down into a quiet anticipation. In August 1992, the Department of the Army issued another memorandum from Tammie Dunn which stated: "This is notice that I am proposing to suspend you from work and pay for three days." Tammie went on to state several reasons, none of which had much validity to Carolyn: It was just another form of harassment. In October 1992, another memorandum was issued by Orlo Jensen, Director of Logistics. The subject of the letter was an official reprimand and went on to redundantly cite the same reasons given by Ms. Dunn.

By now Carolyn's nerves were so frayed she could hardly function. What was the point of those seemingly endless notes from superiors? Other employees had performed far below her standards, yet no one she knew was the recipient of constant notices. Perhaps this was the Army's way—they stuffed information into personnel files, pounded nails into a coffin they hoped to close. When she arrived at work each day, she worried it would be her last day on the job.

And then it finally happened in a memorandum dated December 9, 1992. The subject line read "Notice of Proposed Removal. This is notice that it is proposed to remove you from your position of Supply Clerk at Sierra Army Depot." The reasons were listed in detail and the signature was Tammie Dunn's. Although Carolyn had feared this was coming for a while, when she read it in black and white it was traumatizing. How could one woman carry so much disdain for an employee? Especially with one who lived with a disability? Although the notice had been served, the battle would continue. Carolyn would remain in her position until February 1993 per another memorandum. Contacting her old friend and interpreter, Mary Ann, who still resided in Reno, she begged for help. Quick to respond, Mary Ann hired an attorney and the three had a meeting.

Walking into the sparse waiting room, Carolyn was overjoyed when her eyes met Mary Ann's. They hugged and spilt tears over the situation. Signing wildly with her hands, Mary explained they would have an informative meeting with Tom and that he had the credentials to undo the Army's firing. After a short wait, the receptionist ushered the two women into the attorney's office. Tom was seated at his marred oak desk. Looking around the room, she saw few trappings of a successful lawyer: just two bookcases stuffed with legal reference books and another six book cases filled with red client files. Mary Ann introduced Carolyn and began to brief Tom on what had taken place prior to Carolyn's dismissal. Tom's expressions seemed genuine as he listened "So what do you think? Can you save my friend's job? Can you retaliate against the Army? Do we have a good case?"

Tom explained he was unable to address all those questions until he could take time to do some research. He asked the potential client to review a retainer agreement while he began working on her case. As weeks turned into months, Tom's excuses ran thin and he finally gave up the case. Between the communication barrier and the lack of payment from Carolyn, it was all too taxing and time consuming. He withdrew from the case but encouraged her to keep fighting.

Upon receipt of the letter Carolyn was devastated and began crying. She had put so much faith and trust in Tom and he abandoned her. Desperate, Carolyn set up an appointment with a Nevada state congresswomen, but she too was unable to help. She became immersed in a deep depression.

There were other ways to fight the dismissal. She wrote a letter to the Department of Labor asking for benefits under the Federal Employees' Compensation Act due to an emotional condition." The letter acknowledged receipt of her request but was filled with unanswered questions, saying that her letter was not sufficient for the department to make a decision. A claims adjuster asked Carolyn to provide details regarding the basis of the reprimand, the reason for the proposed removal, the reasons for the suspension, an explanation for insubordination and a comprehensive medical report. Although the Department of Labor demanded much greater detail and an inspection of all her medical issues, she was willing to respond to their demands and she began the arduous process of rewriting her original request for the benefits package.

In the meantime, the EEOC had been sending letters to Sierra Army Base, from the director down to various underlings. All those letters did was to widen the animosity between Carolyn and her employer. Many of the notices required lengthy responses and substantial reasons for the reaction to Carolyn. When supervisors were forced to defend their actions it ruffled their feathers. Blaming the entire situation on the employee was expedient.

In August 1993, Carolyn received a note from the EEOC stating her appeal for benefits was premature and that she could file a new appeal. She needed to file a formal complaint with the EEOC, something only an attorney could do. But since her attorney had resigned from the case, she had to find another lawyer. Grabbing her coat, she leashed the dog and took a long walk into the serene mountains. She would come up with a plan to answer the EEOC. The cool wind sliced into her face. Walking farther on the rugged paths, her mind reflected on the letter and how she could fight her way to winning the benefits she so rightfully deserved. One woman, a woman with a disability, was taking on the entire system. As she walked along the rocky path, she vowed to fight. She would find a lawyer, someone who believed in her cause. There were some good guys out there. All she had to do was find one.

Relying on her savings, she was able to support her modest lifestyle. Changing into a pair of wool pants and a pink cashmere sweater, she applied makeup to her windblown face, brushed out the crunched waves in her hair and prepared for another weekend of socializing. She drove to the laundromat, deposited coins and detergent into the industrial washer, glanced through a magazine and then tossed the clothing into the dryer. An hour later, the sky had transitioned from daylight to twilight. Folding the clean clothing, she stuffed it into the trunk of the car and drove to the bar where a large group of deaf friends had gathered. Her mood instantly perked up. In this bar, she had a bevy of relationships that would support whatever moves she decided to make; here was a group of friends who accepted her deafness. In that moment, whatever hardships she might endure, would be tempered with the love of friends. They toasted Friday night and the beginning of the weekend. The slopes, covered with a fresh layer of pristine dry snow, were on the agenda for the next morning. They agreed to meet early, break for lunch and return to the lodge for late afternoon happy hour. Dinner would end the day as they gathered around a huge stone fireplace exchanging candid thoughts, thoughts that only they could relate to. Communication between the hearing and the deaf was not exact; there were imperfections in translation. But after years of bonding the group of friends had cemented a clear understanding of the subtleties in their thoughts. That was the power that drew this group, and numerous other groups around the country, together. A perfect meeting of the minds.

At midnight Carolyn rose from the floor, waved to the group, grabbed her warm parka and drove the dark empty road home to her trailer. A full day of exercising, socializing, eating and drinking and she was exhausted. Her spirits renewed, she dreamed of fighting for her rights and for the rights of all the deaf; their lives were riddled with endless obstacles. She wasn't going to sit back and allow the Army to steamroll her life.

Her nerves were beyond frazzled and she requested leave with pay due to the constant harassment. The Army was quick to respond and on March 1993, Sherrie Keith, Chief Deputy Property Division, promptly turned down the request: "The purpose of this letter is to inform you that the statement furnished by Dr. Perkins is not sufficient to support a request for continued sick leave. If you choose not to return to work you will be carried in an Absent Without Leave status." Yet another blow to Carolyn, who could hardly work in such a strained environment. Adding fuel to the fire, a couple of days later she received a letter from the U.S. Department of Labor reiterating the same response: "After reviewing the Compensation Act which you filed for an emotional condition. The materials which you have submitted to date have been reviewed and this is not sufficient for this office to determine whether you are eligible for the benefits. If you feel that your illness resulted from being treated in a discriminatory manner by your employer, please provide specific descriptions of all practices, and incidents which affected your condition."

Carolyn was left to draft another lengthy description of the set of circumstances. There were reams of documents and testimony where the conditions had been clearly stated. Rummaging through piles of testimony, she extracted several pages, made copies and offered a response to that letter. The process seemed endless, leaving her feeling alone. She promptly responded

At the end of July 1994, Carolyn received notice from Ronald Vossler, civilian personal officer, regarding her absence from the workplace. (She had already received numerous notices of her impending dismissal). In it he stated, "You are still an employee of the Depot and we must report that to the EEOC. If you feel you are unable to return to duty and would like to resign I have enclosed a request for Personnel action. If you do not wish to resign and are still unable to return to work for medical reasons, you must submit medical documentation from a physician." It elaborated on approved reasons for leave, none of which contained psychological justifications. The only acceptable reasons for absence were due to a physical condition, and she had none. She would never satisfy Mr. Vossler's demands.

Carolyn wrote a letter to U.S. Senator Barbara Boxer, requesting help fighting the discrimination claim against the Army. Reaching out to one of the most powerful persons in California, she hoped her pleadings for equality would be answered.

In mid-October, 1994, the Department of Labor responded that Carolyn's claim was denied and reconsideration was also denied. This denial was punctuated in another letter sent at the end of the month: "The District Office has completed the study of your case and no basis has been found to modify the decision of the office. The evidence submitted in support of the application is not sufficient to warrant modification and is hereby DENIED," signed by D. Shultz, reconsideration examiner. Several pages were attached as evidence for the denial, which constituted a strong defeat for Carolyn's case. A couple of weeks later, she was surprised by a letter generated from U.S. Senator Barbara Boxer to Ms. Donna Onodera, district director of the U.S. Department of Labor, which gave concern over the handling and outcome of the claimant's case: "Caroline has recently contacted our office with additional concerns. Please address Caroline's concern and forward your response to Cynthia Olivia."

Tears of joy welled up in Carolyn's eyes. A chance! That surely would be enough to alter the denials of so many people. Maybe now they would take notice of her case and see how the Army had mistreated her. She wasn't going to allow her life to be judged by a few; she would fight and use the power the average citizen had a right to use. Perhaps that one letter would be enough to undo all the wrongs and allow her case to go forward, or at least allow her to collect some form of compensation. Defeat was finally replaced by hope; Senator Boxer had jumped into the ring to help her out.

Someone powerful was on her side, but she knew this would not be enough. Armed with the letter, she began searching for an attorney who would take her case pro bono, or wait until the case was resolved to receive payment. With the backing of Barbara Boxer's office there had to be some hungry attorney who would fight for Carolyn's cause. After making a series of calls, she signed a retainer agreement with Attorney Brian W. Varner, who practiced in Sacramento. It was the standard retainer agreement where each pledged responsibly to each other for the duration of the case. In mid-December, 1998, a letter was generated from U.S.

Department of Labor acknowledging the formal complaint, but there was one major problem; Attorney Varner filed the suit after the statute of limitations had run out. The case was no longer valid, and was tossed off the court docket. With a meager understanding of legalese, when Carolyn read the letter from a Senior Investigator with the State Bar of California she clearly understood and was furious.

PRIVALEGED AND CONFIDENTIAL

December 10, 1998
Re: Respondent: Brian W Varner
Case No.: 97 0 17615

Dear Caroline:

The State Bar of California has been actively investigating Brian Varner in the captioned matter in which you are the complainant. We are writing to advise you that on June 5, 1998, the State Bar Court ordered that Respondent be disbarred. This means that Brian Varner will no longer be entitled to practice law in California.

There had to be a way to keep fighting. After researching the law, with assistance, she discovered a statute stating that a claimant cannot be punished for their attorney's failure to file documentation on a timely basis. With that information, she sent a letter to Wally Herger, U.S. Congressman, in hopes of reopening the case. Carolyn stated, "I am seeking your help in getting my case re-opened for reconsideration with enough time to obtain new legal counsel who will be able to present my evidence in a proper and timely manner." She hoped there would be a response forthcoming and that it would be in her favor.

In the interim, Brian Varner was disbarred by the State of California. Not only did he fail to file Carolyn's case in a timely manner, but he had failed several others as well. His job, as set forth in the retainer, was to file her case and in the manner as stated by law in the State of California. His failure to do so destroyed her case as well as many others. Because of his actions, many of the cases were thrown out of court. He never bothered to notify any of his clients of this situation.

A response was forthcoming from Wally Herger. He wrote, "In an effort to be of assistance to you, I have contacted the office of Workers' Compensation and requested they respond to me regarding your reconsideration of your file." She felt her case was still viable despite Varner's disbarment and the untimely filing of her case. Time would tell; she would need patience, which she had when it came to matters of law. She would doggedly pursue the discrimination case. She not only owed it to herself, but to all the deaf who had been in the same situation. The only person she could truly trust was herself; it was she and she alone who would make that happen. Compelled, perhaps obsessed, whenever notice of a defeat was held in her hands, she researched alternatives until someone somewhere would listen to her story. With ample time on her side and an intellect, she continued to seek help. She feared no one; she had already faced her worst fears. She was undaunted.

Opening the small post office box, she spied an official looking letter and immediately tore it open. It was from the State Bar of California. Scanning through the three short paragraphs she laughed when they advised her she could sue her former attorney for any fees he had collected regarding the discrimination case. Caressing the envelope, she presumed there would be plenty of lawyers standing in line to sue an apple gone rotten.

On August 24, 2003, she received a cryptic letter form John T. Doolittle, U.S. Representative: "I wanted to let you know that I have contacted officials with the Department of the Army and requested that they look into this matter for you. Although normal response time for most agencies is 30 days you can be assured that I will be back in contact with you as soon as I have received a response." Holding up the letter, she shook her head. The discrimination suit began with the Army in 1994. Here it was nine years later and she felt as if she were still fighting her way out of a paper bag. Would this ever end?

She sat at the small kitchen table staring out the dusty window. Her house has been leveled and now she is reduced to living in what was once a two-car garage. After numerous alterations, the small space became habitable and she rented it out for a small sum each month. With the condemnation notice from the city, there was no alternative. She ousted the unreliable renter of the refurbished space, packed up her belongings and squeezed into it herself. On that Friday morning, as she continued staring at the sun's rays lighting up the sky, her mind wandered back to the insanity of the Army and the insanity of the people who worked at the base. She remembered a letter. "You will not be rude to me! You will have a counseling session for being rude," wrote Sherrie Keith. "Carolyn threw papers at Tammie Dunn!" Even if that were true, which it wasn't, the letter resembled a note written by an immature preschooler. With a lot of time on her hands, Sherrie put together a ridiculous letter. It was she who needed the counseling. As Carolyn continued to ponder the absurdity of the message, it was easy to surmise who was the crazy person. The juvenile behavior left her wondering why she cared so much, why she kept fighting the discrimination lawsuit. But then again it was those very people, like Sherri, who pushed her forward. The pettiness, the lack of understanding and the inability to see beyond their own thoughts, was the fuel that moved Carolyn forward. She had to be tougher and smarter than they were. She would keep fighting.

As she continued reflecting, another poignant memory surfaced, one documented by a fellow co-worker who observed management's treatment: "I observed Carolyn's supervisors passing her notes. On one occasion, I observed a supervisor talking to her and then writing something down on paper and walking away without waiting for a response. On another occasion, I observed her in the supervisor's office without an interpreter. I can remember Carolyn telling me she couldn't understand. Looking back at the time that I worked at the Army Depot, I feel management did not go out of their way to provide a good working environment for Carolyn," signed Donna Alexander. It was painfully clear to Carolyn's colleagues that she was treated unfairly, yet no one could explain why.

Another letter popped into Carolyn's memory, one written by Kathryn Godwin. "I do remember that while [Carolyn] was there working under me, she always worked hard to try to learn the job and do anything she could to do the job. She didn't understand the supply regulations and frankly neither did I, since they are very complicated and difficult to understand. While I was teaching her supply tasks, she was very interested in learning all she could learn and did her best at the jobs I gave her."

There were people who supported her, who believed in her and stood up for her ability to do the job, but those supervisors didn't bang the drum loudly enough to get the attention Carolyn needed.

This thought was followed by a memory of "Rules for Carolyn," composed by D. Alejandro. "You must ask Tammie or Sherrie for an interpreter and you must tell them what you want an interpreter for. You cannot tell the interpreter where to go or what to. You cannot call the interpreter as you must first obtain the permission from Tammie or Sherrie. The interpreter is here to help you communicate and not here to advise. And lastly the interpreter is not a teacher." Of course, the catch was that neither Tammie nor Sherrie would approve the interpreter. As Carolyn continued ruminating over those thoughts, she couldn't help but draw a sly smile. *Those people had a lot of time to kill. Why were some supervisors so supportive of my work while others were so cruel? Maybe it all came down to a lack of understanding and inability to accept a person with a hearing disability.*

She stopped daydreaming. Her stomach was growling and she needed to eat. Her three cats rubbed against her legs. Their food bowl had been licked clean. She stood up and lumbered across the plywood floor, shook the bag of cat food and replenished the metal bowl. She couldn't hear their thankful meows, but the wave of their tails let her know they were happy.

Chapter 14

After a decade, Carolyn grew tired of her surroundings and tired of driving through the small town and seeing the Army Depot Base. Life centered on fighting those people, so it would be better to be closer to the people who could help her win her case. After reviewing her options, she hitched her trailer to her car and drove to Oroville, California, home to the Oroville Dam and Lake Oroville. With a population around 15,000, she had scanned the newspapers and found the town affordable for her meager income. As she slowly cruised through the small downtown historic center, she located a side street and parked the car and trailer in a huge parking lot. She began walking to the main street with her dog on a leash and then up and down numerous side streets. It was the quintessential small town with small stores dotting the main streets and a large brick building where the courthouse and city records were housed.

Meandering through the empty streets she felt comfortable and safe but at that moment she had no idea where she would live. At the far corner of Main Street stood a real estate office. It was open for business and she tentatively walked in. The clerk realized this customer was deaf and handed her a pen and small writing tablet. Carolyn scribbled a note asking for the trailer parks in the area. Although the real estate office would not make any money off the advice, the clerk looked up the information and printed out several parks within a ten-mile radius. Handing over a map, she smiled and Carolyn departed with her dog in tow. Returning to the trailer, she slowly eased out of the parking lot and drove north to the first park, which was three miles from the center of town. The entrance sign read "Golden Park Trailer Park." It wasn't golden, but the place seemed welcoming enough.

There were nearly one-hundred trailers parked in neat clean rows and numerous tall evergreens shaded the clean streets. If there was any noise, it didn't distract her. Sighing, she thought it would be wonderful to live among people after spending ten years in an isolated spot. Perhaps she would be able to make a new set of friends.

Driving farther into the property, she stopped the car when she spied the manager's office. It was mid-day and someone should be available. Knocking on the trailer door she stood back when a man thrust open the screen door and looked at her with annoyance. At once Carolyn began signing with her hands and pointed to her trailer. He was quick to understand she was unable to hear and used hand signals to relay he would be right back. A couple of minutes later he handed her the monthly rental agreement and signaled her to follow him to available empty spaces. Carolyn trailed behind the manager and was pleasantly surprised when he showed her three spaces at the end of the farthest row. Pointing out the utility hook-ups, he continued walking around the park pointing out picnic tables, a children's play area, a dog-walk, and an above -ground pool.

After the tour they returned to the manager's trailer and Carolyn signed a contract for six months. They shook hands and she drove to the designated spot. After connecting the utilities and unhitching the trailer from her car, she was home. It had been a decade since she had lived in a close-knit community. This was a welcome change, or at least she hoped so. Preoccupied with the new living arrangements, the stubborn memories of St. John's had been temporarily shoved into the background. But then again, she hadn't yet spent her first night sleeping in the trailer park. The sun was slipping over the horizon, the dog was comatose on the floor and suddenly she felt a yawn coming on. She was sleepy too and began to prepare for bed. It was the first time in a decade when she wouldn't have to traipse water to the trailer. She took a lengthy warm shower, shampooed her hair, downed a glass of ice water and collapsed onto the bed. She prayed sleep would come and peace with it.

But she soon discovered it didn't matter where she slept, or when she slept; those hidden demons raced through her mind jockeying for attention. Waking up in the middle of the night, she was dripping wet as thoughts of sexual abuse jarred her. She screamed, she wept, she swore, but nothing undid the dark experiences. Granted, she had moved to Oroville to be closer to services and people who would help her, but she had hoped that fresh scenery and a change of environment would evaporate the evil thoughts. Padding to the bathroom she wiped the sweat off her face, and returned to bed tossing and turning until the sun rose for the start of a new day.

Downtown Oroville was a lengthy walk, but it provided for all basic needs and was an excuse for a long daily hike. The six-mile round-trip would keep both her and the dog in shape. Living here she would be a short drive to her attorney's office in downtown Sacramento, and deaf services. She felt certain she had made the right choice. After the morning constitutional, she grabbed the car keys in search of a grocery store. Before the move, she had whittled down the provisions in the pantry. It was time to restock. Filling the shopping cart with dog food, a variety of vegetables, fruit, pasta and snacks, she had all she needed. She also grabbed a bottle of shower gel, a luxury she hadn't allowed herself in over a decade. Remembering how delicious the soothing warm water felt, she wanted to make that event a daily habit. No more lugging up gallons of winter to outside receptacles.

Commencing a new stage in her life, she began a daily routine devoted to creating a happier healthier lifestyle. Each day she and the dog kept to an early morning regiment of walking into town and back, regardless of the weather. She ate well, eliminating caffeine, alcohol, and sodas, while concentrating on a vegetarian diet. As the days rolled into months, her body became stronger yet nothing she did erased the memories of her childhood.

On a bright sunny morning, Carolyn pulled the leash from the kitchen drawer but her dog didn't move from his prone position; he was too sick. The dreaded time had come. Putting the leash on his collar, she drove him to the veterinarian's office and a simple shake of the vet's head confirmed it was time to ease the dog's pain. The cancer had done its damage and there was no reason to commit this animal to another day of pain. Crying, Carolyn undid the leash, kissed her dog goodbye and drove back home. She almost wished for a rainy day because her heart felt gray with sadness.

With so much pain in her heart, she opted for an alternative walk near the lake. The breezes were cooler and the view prettier as she walked near the muddy bank. Ahead was a large silver-streaked husky walking alone with no leash and no collar. Clapping her hands together the dog galloped over to her side and licked her hand. No doubt this was a trained dog that had either escaped from home or, possibly was dumped out of a moving car. Carolyn could form very few sounds and after a long walk, she was able to yell out, "Sissy." The husky turned his head and from that moment on the stray dog had a new name and a new life. After the death of her dog she felt that this stray was a sign from the heavens; a human and a dog who needed each other. Returning to the trailer, both she and the dog were exhausted. Quickly filling the water and food dishes, the stray inhaled every morsel, drank all the water and dropped to the floor for a long snooze. There was a seamless introduction of Sissy to the household and Carolyn welcomed the added security of a big, strong dog. The husky had a difficult time communicating with its new owner but as time wore on, Sissy adapted to her hand signals and unusual sounds. Cocking his ears, he looked into her eyes and eventually figured out what was happening. Carolyn gave the new dog endless love and always made sure his dishes were filled with food and water. She didn't know how long the dog had lived on his own, and giving him a sense of security would wash away the trauma.

The neighbors at the trailer park weren't as warm and fuzzy as one might expect them to be in this remote community. No one came knocking on Carolyn's door welcoming her with a cake or a homemade platter of cookies. Instead, everyone kept their distance and so did she. After a long life of abuse, she trusted no one and didn't bother trying to make friends. Instead she built a fence in the front of her trailer; she said it was to hold the dog but in fact it was to deter the neighbors from coming near her home. There wasn't another fence in the entire community but that didn't stop her from erecting it. The landlord ignored it and none of the renters complained, so the manager turned a blind eye. All the tenants were at the bottom of the socioeconomic ladder: drugs, alcoholism and gambling were rampant. One small fence was the least of his problems compared to collecting rent and keeping the park afloat.

Carolyn was a force to be reckoned with when it came to the rights of the deaf. An advocate, she was surprised that the local hospital in Oroville had no interpreter available for the patients. In a newspaper article dated August 1, 2002, the headline read: *Deaf Woman Forces Hospital to Change.*

"After years of trying to convince Oroville Hospital staff that it needed a highly skilled sign language interpreter to effectively treat deaf patients like her, Carolyn turned elsewhere. Three civil rights complaints filed with two federal agencies eventually led her to a powerful ally in Sacramento— Assistant US Attorney Michael Hirst. The prosecutor signed off Wednesday on a 14-page agreement between the government and the hospital owner Golden Valley Health Network calling for a sweeping revision of policy regarding the care of deaf and hearing-impaired patients. No one should be forced to make medical decisions without a full understanding of what's involved. This agreement ensures that in Oroville they now have the same opportunities. Carolyn explained that is takes a top-level sign interpreter to deal with medical terms and intricate diagnosis that are a part of the communications between a physician and a patient. Among other changes the hospital will provide free auxiliary aids and services which will include listening devices, real time transcriptional services and interpreters. Someone will always be available to assist these patients. In addition, physicians and staff will be trained on treating deaf and hearing-impaired."

Smiling, Carolyn reread the article, and stuffed it into a metal box filled with important documents and memorabilia. A small victory, but it was worth the fight. She fought and won the right to fair treatment in the Oroville Hospital. The repercussions of this one court case would ripple, sending a message to other hospitals across America; treat the deaf and hearing-impaired with respect and consideration. Winning a small battle in the war for equal opportunity catapulted Carolyn's sense of self-worth. Standing up for the hearing disabled and winning a court case against a huge corporation encouraged her to continue fighting.

Sacramento, a short drive away, became her social world and the place where deaf advocate services would help her in her fight with the EEOC. The trailer park was only a place to sleep and provide inexpensive utilities. Turning over the engine, Carolyn traveled into town with a short grocery list, a basket of dirty laundry and an optimistic notion that her attorney would have some good news regarding her case. Two years and there had been no movement; she would be strong and hold him to his lofty promises. Although she had been notified by the State Bar of California of Varner's disbarment, today she would walk into his office and demand answers and she would not leave until he talked with her. She did not realize that disbarment meant an end to attorney services; she was certain he was still sitting in his leather chair, feet propped up on the desk starring pensively into a pile of pleadings.

After knocking on the door, she let herself into the empty waiting room. It smelled musty and was barren except for a desk and chair. No one was around: no telephones, empty glasses, or filled trash cans. The top of the receptionist's desk had a fine layer of dust as if no one had sat there in weeks. She knocked on Brian's door and there was no response, so she let herself into the room and it was just as barren as the lobby. She began walking around and spied a court document hidden under the local newspaper. It was an official notice that Brian Varner had been disbarred from practicing law in the state of California. Reading through the long document she could see that her lawyer had done some awful things, the most relevant being a failure to file Carolyn's case on time. After reading the last word on the last page she screamed. She had moved to Oroville to be closer to her attorney and he was totally negligent; her case had gone nowhere. All those assurances were lies—he never acted on her case and as indicated in the document, he had never acted on several other cases leaving his clients in the wind. *What was she to do? What recourse?* She felt like a fool who had been taken advantage of. *And what about the advocates? Where were they when all of this was occurring?* Inserting the disbarment document into her purse, she hurried out of the office and walked out into the street. Justice seemed to escape her at every turn. Disbarment, she surmised, meant the end of the attorney's practice. He was forced to close his office and face public humiliation.

Walking back to the car, she inserted the key into the ignition and continued with her errands before she headed home. She was in no mood to socialize nor complain to her advocates. It appeared as if the entire world had let her down. A sour mood permeated her thoughts, all wrought by a lying, inept lawyer, who even the State of California no longer wanted. Driving up to the trailer, she unlatched the gate to the fence. The dog rushed to greet her, lapping at her heels and jumping in the air. Sissy knew those big brown bags held food and treats. After emptying the contents of the trunk, Carolyn wrote out the rent check and walked over to the manager's trailer. She ruminated over the loss of her lawyer and was too inattentive to observe what was happening in front of her. She gently knocked on the screen door and the manager's dog leaped out of the trailer, raced over to Carolyn, jumped up and bit her on the nose. Hearing the scream, the manager flung open the screen door to see his tenant holding her bloody nose. Grabbing a dirty towel from the kitchen sink, he gently pressed it onto the stream of blood, took her arm, escorted her into his dusty truck and drove to the local emergency room.

The medical staff had taken care of many dog bites, but rarely one that involved a nose. After cleaning the wound, giving her a tetanus shot, and something for the pain, the on-call surgeon stitched up her nose, dressed the wound and sent her home with a list of instructions. All she could think about on the drive home was "This really rounds out my day!"

The ways of the law were becoming second nature to Carolyn and she decided to sue the manager for the dog bite. It was an easy fix to pay off the medical bills and show him that he needed to control his mongrel. The court ordered that all medical costs be paid and there was a meager amount ordered for pain and suffering. She was more successful with this case than the one for which she retained a lawyer. Whenever she was near the manager's office, she walked on eggshells and he in turn collected her rent check in person. Carolyn and the dog never crossed paths again.

The balance of the day was a blur as she sat on the lounger staring at the setting sun, feeling the painful throbbing in her nose. Although she was armed with medication she preferred a hot cup of tea and a shower. When her head finally hit the pillow, deep sleep never arrived. Between the anger she felt for her attorney, that stupid dog, her landlord and the advocates, her nerves were live wires.

By the end of the year, the current manager of the trailer park had been sacked, replaced by a meaner, nastier version who insisted that rent be paid on time and all the rules stringently followed. He walked from trailer to trailer introducing himself, jotting down notes and scowling. A week later Carolyn received a cryptic note explaining that she must remove the fence or she would be removed from the park. The new manager didn't realize who he was dealing with—a fighter who had become accustomed to never accepting defeat. In retaliation, she stopped paying the rent.

A few days later as she was standing in her front yard, she ducked when a young teenager tossed oranges at her and her dog. Grabbing one of the oranges she threw it back at the kid, returned to her trailer, and began thinking about moving. Unable to sleep she stood at the window and stared up at the midnight sky. Emotions kept her awake as she tried to deal with the uncomfortable situation. Handling tactile problems was easy, but intangible feelings were oftentimes beyond her ability to grasp. She struggled to understand human behavior when it came to motive; it was something that had been lost in her youth.

Her eyes drifted down toward the front yard and then over to a cluster of trees. A person was opening front doors, entering several trailers and leaving with bundles of stuff in their arms. She watched as the robber went from trailer to trailer repeating the same act. Dressed completely in black with a black cap and jacket, it was impossible to discern if it was a man or woman. Regardless, there was a thief among the inhabitants and that thief needed to be caught. Glancing over at the bedside clock, it read 3:00 am. Dare she call the police? Picking up the phone she typed in the robbery and prayed a police car would arrive but it never did. In the morning, she tried again but the police still refused to investigate. Disgusted, she had had enough. Flipping open her laptop she struck the keys and began searching for a way out of the neighborhood. With her modest income she knew the pickings would be slim but there had to be a better, safer place. It was only a matter of time before that robber would appear at her doorstep. Deafness would be a hindrance and the dog might not be strong enough to deter the robber. It was time to get out.

The following evening, she found it impossible to sleep. Again, she stood staring out the window wondering if the robber would reappear or come crashing through her own front door. Out of the corner of her eye she spied a bright flash. Turning toward the light she witnessed a car had burst into flames. Again, she called the police and again no one bother to come. She felt as if she were living in a lawless society. It was true that the population at the trailer park lived well below the poverty line but that shouldn't translate into being ignored by emergency services.

Perhaps the straw that broke the camel's back was a letter from the U.S. Department of Labor informing her that her request for reconsideration had been denied; she would not be receiving compensation for her fight with the EEOC. There was a dim light at the end of the tunnel: "If you disagree with this decision denying reconsideration of your case, you may prepare a request by the Employees' Compensation Appeals Board." For this option to be successful she knew a seasoned attorney was the only viable option and her funds were hemorrhaging at a fast pace. Giving up wasn't her style but perhaps it was time to move on.

When the sun warmed up the air, she leashed the dog and began the routine three-mile walk into town. Between the fresh air and the joy she received from Sissy, the walk always had a positive effect on her mood. She wondered how many other deaf or disabled people suffered due to their circumstances and how hard it was to make a living when you are burdened with a disability. Thinking back to her deaf friends and acquaintances, she couldn't think of one who wasn't struggling financially; making a living with a disability was hard. True, her education was lacking, but deafness was frustrating and limited her opportunities. The one place where she felt equal was at her computer where hearing was unnecessary. All communications were typed and read, with no need for sound to be able to discern messages. She thought about the future and how deafness might not be such a curse; that it would be possible to be highly successful if you knew your way around computers. She would concentrate on that thought as she hiked into the city. Putting a smile on her face she hooked the leash around a pole and headed into the bakery to purchase a loaf of freshly baked bread. The smell was intoxicating—it was one of her senses she could fully enjoy.

Chapter 15

On January 13, 2004, the U.S. District Court of Northern California stamped a case number on Carolyn's pleading for appointment of counsel under the Civil Rights Act of 1964. This was accompanied with a Complaint for Employment Discrimination. She had done her homework, researched the options and discovered she could still fight the fight if she had the right ammunition. The courts answered within thirty days and on February 10, 2004, issued an Order Dismissing the Complaint and denying the case to proceed through the courts. The Court also requested an Order Denying the Plaintiff's Request for Appointment of Counsel. The end of the road had finally arrived.

Opening her email, Carolyn read an intriguing note sent from her sister: "A friend of mine found the name Jeff Anderson, an attorney who represented child abuse cases. This caught my attention and I began to research the attorney." Logging onto the website it read, "You are not alone. Seeking justice for survivors of childhood abuse is more than a job—it is our cause." Rereading the quote, Carolyn was surprised that someone, especially an attorney, knew anything about the horrors she suffered as a child. She began reviewing the website, the Child Victims Act, the attorney's background, areas of expertise and his fight for the sexually abused. When she read, "Jeff Anderson & Associates pioneered the use of civil litigation to seek justice for survivors of child sexual abuse and is recognized as one of the nation's premier law firms to represent survivors of clergy sexual abuse," she was shocked that someone understood what she had gone through and was willing to punish those who stole her childhood. The lawyer's office was in Wisconsin, so she wondered if he was aware of the problems at St. John's. Had anyone complained about the abuse? She had been a victim of sexual abuse and witnessed others who had been abused, but in all those years did someone come forth? Did someone feel they had a right to get back at the abusive clergy? Was someone brave enough to come forward with allegations? Was it more than one person? Her mind raced. There was only one way to find out. Picking up the phone, she placed a call to Jeff Anderson's law office and began a conversation with his secretary. Surprised the conversation flowed so easily, the secretary explained that in fact Mr. Anderson had begun a lawsuit with St. John's, and with so many deaf clients that they set up a system that expeditiously interpreted the conversations.

"How many people have come forward?"

"I can't give you names," responded the secretary, "but I can tell you that there are over 300 people who have put their names on the Complaint."

"That many?" typed in Carolyn, "I am surprised. Can you please give me some details? How can I become a part of this lawsuit? I was there, I saw what the nuns did to my schoolmates and I know what they did to me. I have been living with this nightmare my entire life and now after decades someone has decided to punish those awful people. I can't believe this."

The secretary sent over a list of questions and asked Carolyn to complete the information and return it back to their office as quickly as possible. She elaborated that at the end of the lawsuit, if they should win, which they felt quite confident about, Carolyn would be entitled to a share in the money awarded by the court. This piqued her interest. What did she have to lose? She had been living with the pangs of abuse forever; it wasn't as if she had put it aside and forgotten about the pain. By elaborating the details, it wouldn't further distress her psyche; it was already constantly embedded in her mind.

When the next email appeared on her screen, she immediately began reading. The first priority was to sign the retainer. After supplying several pleadings to the courts, she had become competent in legalese and readily understood the language in the retainer. There were no costs to the plaintiff. As that was her main worry, she felt confident when she signed the one-page document, scanned it and returned it to the office. The secretary then forwarded a lengthy questionnaire which would take days to complete. As Carolyn began typing the responses, she felt her heart pounding. There were a lot of details to supply. Reliving her abuse on paper was an agony; all her thoughts on the subject had been experienced through her memories. In that moment, someone who had an intrinsic interest in her life wanted to see those memories in black and white. Although so much of the abuse was at the top of her memory, the detailed questions forced her into reliving the smallest details.

It was days before she returned the completed responses to Jeff Anderson but she wanted to comply and give detailed answers. She wanted to let him, and now the entire universe, know the hell she had endured at the hands of the clergy at St. John's. When she finally sent the response, it wasn't cathartic; it was merely detailed answers to their questions. But, oh, had she experienced so much more than she wrote. *Someday this horrific story will come out and the world will see how the Catholic clergy took sexual advantage of all of us young innocent kids. How we gave up our youth, dashed our dreams of love and for some evaporated any hope of finding happiness.*

Prying open several large plastic boxes she began digging through piles of documents, testimony, notes and emails, anything and everything that would help win the case Jeff Anderson was proposing. She came across the following statement written by a psychiatrist. As part of her battle with the EEOC, they demanded a psychological evaluation and insisted that she see a psychiatrist. It was a humiliating experience the results of which she wanted kept confidential. After rereading the synopsis, she cried because all of it was true and it dictated how her life had evolved. The effect of childhood abuse took a heavy toll in every aspect of her life:

Nature of the Sexual Abuse:
Carolyn was sexually abused by Fr. Lawrence Murphy, Sister Lois, Sister Rene, Sister Marth and Sister Ethel while she was

a live in student at St. John's School for the Deaf in St. Francis, Wisconsin. Fr. Murphy was a priest and director of St. John's School for the Deaf. Sister Lois, Sister Rene and Sister Ethel were teachers at St. John's School for the Deaf. Sister Martha was a dorm supervisor at St. John's School for the Deaf. The abuse occurred numerous times from approximately 1949-1960.

Fr. Murphy touched Carolyn's hair. Fr. Murphy patted Carolyn on the back and pinched her cheeks. Fr. Murphy hugged Carolyn. Fr. Murphy touched Carolyn's breasts and genitals inside her clothing. Fr. Murphy teased Carolyn and acted like he was playing a game with her. The abuse occurred numerous times. Fr. Murphy told Caroline not to tell anyone. Sister Lois touched Carolyn's breasts while they were bathing. The abuse occurred 3 times. Sister Rene physically abused Carolyn and touched her breasts. Sister Martha touched Carolyn's breasts and vagina while bathing. The abuse occurred numerous times. Sister Ethel hit Carolyn and touched her vagina. All of the abuse occurred on the grounds of St. John's School for the Deaf in St. Francis, Wisconsin.

Impact of the Sexual Abuse
In addition to and including the injuries listed in the proof of claim form, Carolyn has suffered from various physical, emotional and psychological injuries as a result of the abuse. ...

Carolyn struggles with depression and anxiety. Carolyn has had thoughts of suicide and has attempted suicide. She is distracted by thoughts of abuse every day. At times she cannot get it out of her mind. ... Carolyn has dreams, nightmares, flashbacks, and other sleep issues. ... Carolyn has had relationship and intimacy issues. She has had a loss of sexual desire and activity. Carolyn struggles with sexual dysfunction. Carolyn has faith, religion and spirituality issues.

Tossing it into a pile of documents she would later send this to the attorney as fuel for the case. Although many written statements were redundant, a single typed page caught her eye. Cryptic, it described how things were: the statements were as simple as if they were typed by Carolyn's own fingers yet the message was poignant and fraught with heartache of a broken life.

--I learned how to talk, how to communicate, but at night I hid under my covers, felt sick and endured being molested by the nuns.

--Thy put something in my anus, I was crying, it was awful, they screamed at me with their eyes, it was bad.

--I used to cry when my dad came. When I did go home, I cried to stay and not return to that awful place. My parents didn't understand why I was so upset.

=Back at school even when I was just having fun, not doing anything wrong, the nuns would hit me, slap me for no reason, we were told we were little devils. We were sometimes punished, sent to bed with no dinner. They said we were behaving badly.

--the teachers were not educated, no college degree, sometimes only 15 to 17 years old.

-we would see the father come through, patting our heads, saying hi, but they were never around when the nuns beat us.

--some kids would go home over the weekend, but I had to stay there. My home was too far away, couldn't go every weekend. I remember sleeping in a dark room while nuns molested me and others. Those kids that lived near the school were not touched.

She learned to trust and rely on nobody but herself. Until she had contacted Jeff Anderson, she thought she was the only one on the planet who had suffered emotionally from the abuse. Over the years she had acquired numerous deaf friends and acquaintances and never once did a conversation of this magnitude ever come up. She and her colleagues conversed about the hardships of deafness but never delved into sexual abuse. Since she left St. John's, she felt alone in her daily struggle. The revelation that she would join 300 schoolmates made her realize she was not alone and not the only person suffering dire consequences.

Yes, she nodded her head, the notes were cryptic, but if she was asked to describe in a nutshell the abuse that list would be an accurate description. Turning to the mounting pile of rumpled papers, she gathered the pages, bundled them in a large paper bag, drove to the hardware store and made a copy for the attorney. The copies went into a large mailing envelope, then she added postage and slipped the package into the drop box. Over the years she had learned that justice was slow to arrive and patience was needed. The consolation, the thought that brightened her day and the days to come, was that she was no longer alone in her suffering, that hundreds of others had suffered at the hands of the clergy and were willing to come forward.

Jeff Anderson was shepherding a group of abused clients into a large and soon-famous lawsuit that would affect the Catholic Church, one of the richest and most powerful institutions on the face of our planet. He was confident and had no doubt the final Complaint would end up on a polished table staring into the eyes of the Pope and his army of lawyers. As in the past, Jeff was aware the Church would try to hide the lawsuit under luxurious antique carpets, dismissing it as frivolous and unwarranted, but he wouldn't give up; there was too much at stake. Hundreds of abused children were too many to ignore. He entered the litigation ring, sparring with the most powerful men on earth. The Catholic Church had to bear the consequences of its actions.

The case crept through the court system in Wisconsin. At every turn, Anderson pushed the suit until a decision was handed down, and it came in the package of a hefty payout to the plaintiffs. Carolyn, like most of her fellow plaintiffs, did not testify in court; rather, videos and written testimony were offered as discovery. One can't help but wonder what it must have been like to sit on the jury and view all those children, now adults, separate and apart, telling similar stories of sexual abuse. The surprise and disgust on the faces of the jury members as they were presented with the evidence must have wreaked havoc with the defense attorneys. In the end, the jury knew no amount of cash award could ever undo the heinous crimes of the clergy, but the award served as notice that those crimes would not be tolerated in our society. Preying on the young and the disabled was not what the Catholic Church, nor our educators, are supposed to do. The Church and our school system are supposed to be safe havens, places where all our children can feel safe while learning. There were no criminal charges, and no single person was ever sent to jail. The guilty individuals escaped being singled out. The penalty for their sins was cash to the victims from the Church.

Few were privy to the final verdict, the amount of the monetary award, which was sealed to protect the innocent. The Catholic Church of Milwaukee was aghast. They did not have the means to pay the award and so they reached out to the higher-ups for advice. In the end, lacking liquidity, they had no choice but to file for Chapter 11 bankruptcy. But because the court award was based upon restitution, there was no escape. A sum of $21 million had to be paid to the plaintiffs. The Catholic Church was forced to cough up the money. Once all the Plaintiffs and creditors had entered their Proof of Claims, the Trustee approved a payback plan which is then approved by the Judge and the plaintiffs then receive payment. When anyone or any company files bankruptcy, it is public knowledge. In this case the Catholic Church of Milwaukee had to endure the public humiliation of filing for bankruptcy.

Holding the letter from Jeff Anderson, Carolyn was circumspect on the allocation of her share of the court-ordered award. When reviewing the substantial award, she realized that this must be shared amongst all plaintiffs. At first glance, what seemed to be a life-changing award, when divided up among the group of plaintiffs, became a paltry amount of money. Perhaps there was some relief in knowing that no other innocent children would suffer at the hands of

St. John's clergy, and perhaps that should be enough. Yet a lifetime dogged with the nightmares of sexual abuse could never be erased, nor could the affects the abuse had upon Carolyn's life. Those relentless memories bubbled to the surface, causing pain and suffering that was nightmarish. No matter how Carolyn lives out her life, during the clarity of the afternoon to the somnolent peace of morning sleep, those memories of sexual abuse clutter her mind, disturb her sanity and shackle up any opportunity to love. Trusting another human being had become beyond her ability. "If you ask me who is the most important person in my life, the one person I can truly rely upon, I would have to say it is myself. Too many times I have put my trust in others and ended up hurt and disappointed."

The front page of the Chicago Tribune's headlines summed up Jeff Anderson's lawsuit: *Vatican Served with Court Papers in Wisconsin Abuse Case*. This was accompanied with several photos of male clergy and a lengthy story. A picture of the church was displayed with the caption: "The lawsuit filed nearly a year ago in federal court alleged Pope Benedict XVI and two other top Vatican officials knew about allegations of sexual abuse at St. John's and called off internal punishment of the accused priest, the Rev. Lawrence Murphy."

Because of the magnitude and notoriety of the lawsuit, Anderson announced a forum to help survivors deal with the hardships of sexual abuse received at St John's. He reserved rooms at the Crowne Plaza Hotel in Milwaukee and sent out notices to the survivors, families and supporters. He believed it was important to share and commiserate over the ramifications of the church's behavior. Sharing experiences might help ease the pain, or at the very least, allow the victims a chance to understand they were not alone in their suffering. The forum included Terry Kohut, a plaintiff who came forward and was featured on a CNN documentary, *What the Pope Knew*, Father Thomas Doyle, a priest who willingly came forward to explain the reality of sexual abuse, and Alisa Cohen-Stein, a clinical social worker specializing in treating the deaf. The Catholic Church could no longer cover up the heinous crimes. Both internal and external sources came forward to expose the truth. They could no longer hide and pretend none of that had happened, and claiming that the young children were making up stories. The Church suffered, but only monetarily; not one individual ever saw the inside of a jail cell. Had the average citizen committed those same crimes, a jury would have sent the perpetrator to prison.

On March 25, 2010, The New York Times ran the headline, *Vatican Declined to Defrock Wisconsin Priest Who Abused Deaf Boys.* "Father Murphy not only was never tried or disciplined by the church's own justice system but also got a pass from the police and prosecutors who ignored reports from his victims. Even as the Pope himself in a letter to Irish Catholics has emphasized the need to cooperate with civil justice in abuse cases, the correspondence seems to indicate that the Vatican's insistence on secrecy has often impeded such cooperation. At the same time the officials' reluctance to defrock a sex abuser shows that on a doctrinal level the Vatican has tended to view the matter in terms of sin and repentance more than crime and punishment. The Vatican's inaction is not unusual. Only 20 percent of the 3,000 accused priests whose cases went to the doctrinal office between 2001 and 2010 were given full church trials."

In its April 12, 2010 issue, *People Magazine* ran an extensive article entitled *Shattered Faith,* asking "Did one Wisconsin priest molest scores of deaf boys? And is the Pope guilty of giving him a free pass? Victims tell *People* how they believe the Catholic Church protected pedophile priests." The article was centered on one victim, Arthur Budzinski, who told an abbreviated version of his experiences at St John's, all of which corroborated Carolyn's story. "He was twelve years old when Fr. Lawrence Murphy called him into a coat closet. It was there, recalls Arthur Budzinski, that the priest molested him. After that, he saw Fr. Murphy come into the boy's dorm at night and put his hands underneath the blankets. The light would glow from the red exit sign and you could see him. 'I'd pull my blanket over my eyes

and cry.' Now Budzinski, one of 200 deaf boys allegedly molested by Fr. Murphy from 1950-1974, is accusing the very
head of the Catholic Church of doing much the same thing:
knowing a horrible truth and yet looking away. In what is
becoming one of the most serious sex scandals to ever rock
the church, the allegations against Fr. Murphy, as well as
charges against priests in Ireland and Germany have all been
linked to Pope Benedict XVI, who oversaw claims as head
of the Vatican's Congregation for the Doctrine of the Faith
from 1981-2005. Several former St. Johns' students said he
preyed on the most vulnerable boys, such as those with no
parents or parents who didn't sign. Dean Weismeller said, I
was sent to his office and told to take off my clothes and play
with myself. Then [Fr. Murphy] did it to me. And at the end
he said 'Amen.' Fr. Murphy eventually admitted to a social
worker that he molested some students but claimed it was
sex education for them. Mr. Budzinski fully admits how the
sexual abuse has destroyed his life and brought him close to
suicide."

Chapter 16

L oving animals is Carolyn's passion; they give her unconditional love and never disappoint. Rescuing dogs solved two problems: giving a dog a loving home and herself a chance to express love and genuine caring. After her last dog died, she collected stray cats, giving them a chance to live a happy, healthy life. In her retirement, cats have given her unabashed love with a minimum of care. She doesn't have to hear their meows to communicate; a simple brush on her leg or a tap on her toe and they tell her what they want. Most often they want to be picked up and held or to play with a toy. They want her attention.

In all that has transpired in her turbulent life, Carolyn does feel the essence of love and has become capable of demonstrating honest love and caring. Although robbed of a childhood and bonds with her parents and siblings, somewhere along the road she internalized the ability to love others and accept love, although cautiously.

Of the hundreds, perhaps thousands, of innocent children abused at St. John's School for the Deaf, why did she become one of the plaintiffs in the complaint? Was it that she felt she had nothing to lose or that this would cause millions around the world to awake to the horrors caused by the Catholic Church? Jeff Anderson made no promises other than the fact he wanted to punish the Catholic Church for its abhorrent behavior, attacking the most vulnerable in our society. Even the God she had been taught to believe in had abandoned her. She became emboldened with the strength to step forward and join the other plaintiffs willing to open up the cloistered walls of St John, shedding light on the atrocities of the clergy. It wasn't just the males, but also the women, the nuns and novices, who committed just as many of the sexual crimes. Disobeying the purity of their vows, the women took as many opportunities as their male counterparts to engage in pedophilia.

The case now settled, Carolyn sits at her computer scouring the internet for coupons and bargains. Her life hasn't changed. She finds little comfort in her share of the award; it was not a life-changing sum of money, but rather a token of the Catholic Church admitting to guilt and the destruction of young lives. Some deep-seated wounds are best left that way, buried in the psyche to be forgotten. In this case, opening up the wounds and demonstrating to the world the crimes that had taken place would help her cope. She discovered she was not alone, that her fellow students suffered just as she did. Joining forces, they attacked one of the oldest, wealthiest, and most powerful institutions on earth and won.

A few renegade tears seep out of the corners of Carolyn's eyes. She had suffered and was still feeling the pangs of the abuse but she no longer suffers alone and she no longer suffers in silence.

Opening a can of cat food, she dumps the contents into a metal bowl, fills up the water dish, gulps down some ice cold water and begins another day. Searching the internet, she wonders what opportunities lie ahead; is there something she can do to advocate for the deaf? Are there any coupons? Any interesting lawsuits? Any new laws to protect the disabled? Will the world implode today? Laughing, she rattles off several emails to friends and family, grabs her sunglasses and goes for a walk in the neighborhood. Every day there are new discoveries.

Carolyn can be defined as a strong independent soul. Her goal was to expose the clergy who stole her innocence and took away her right to live a happy life. When she discovered that so many fellow students joined the lawsuit exposing the clergy she wanted to do more than collect a small sum of money. The sealed details of what the clergy did to the young children will never come to light. Exposing the abominable acts of not just one or two clergy, but the entire staff, took an immense amount of courage.

Respect is often not given to the disabled. Society, harboring prejudices and a lack of understanding, often overlooks the heroes among us. It isn't a bright red cape, surging muscles, or the ability to shoot a gun that makes a hero, but rather exposing the truth and bringing the perpetrators to justice. This is the work of a hero.

Thank you to Carolyn for opening up her heart and memories to expose the worst inhuman behavior from those humans who espouse to be messengers of God.

About the Author

A rlene Krieger was born in Salem, Oregon, a bucolic capital city. After high school, she graduated with a BA in Sociology from the University of Arizona. Moving back east, she obtained a degree in Accounting from the University of Baltimore. Living in New York, she joined her in-laws in developing a designer collection of women's clothing. After decades, they closed shop. Reinventing her career, she obtained a Master's in Education from Kean University and began teaching. When her two children were out of college, she and her spouse pulled up stakes and moved to Las Vegas, where her writing career commenced. *Freedom Twice Lost*, the biography of the only man released from death row from the state of Nevada, was her first book. Her other books include *Heart of a Designer*, *The NiteKings*, *Little Anthony*, *Tony Sacca*, *Cornel Gunther's Coasters*, *Privileged Attorneys*, and *A Las Vegas Affair*. *A Family of Friends*, a novel based upon a revolutionary way of living, is set to be released this year.

CPSIA information can be obtained
at www.ICGtesting.com
Printed in the USA
BVOW09s1502261017

498718BV00018B/372/P